Small Talk Made Simple

31 Techniques to Avoid Social Anxiety & Lead Genuine Conversations

Sidney Neel

© **Copyright 2022 - All rights reserved.**

The content contained within this book may not be reproduced, duplicated or transmitted without direct written permission from the author or the publisher.

Under no circumstances will any blame or legal responsibility be held against the publisher, or author, for any damages, reparation, or monetary loss due to the information contained within this book, either directly or indirectly.

Legal Notice:

This book is copyright protected. It is only for personal use. You cannot amend, distribute, sell, use, quote or paraphrase any part, or the content within this book, without the consent of the author or publisher.

Disclaimer Notice:

Please note the information contained within this document is for educational and entertainment purposes only. All effort has been executed to present accurate, up to date, reliable, complete information. No warranties of any kind are declared or implied. Readers acknowledge that the author is not engaged in the rendering of legal, financial, medical or professional advice. The content within this book has been derived from various sources. Please consult a licensed professional before attempting any techniques outlined in this book.

By reading this document, the reader agrees that under no circumstances is the author responsible for any losses, direct or indirect, that are incurred as a result of the use of the information contained within this document, including, but not limited to, errors, omissions, or inaccuracies.

Table of Contents

INTRODUCTION 1

CHAPTER 1: GETTING STARTED 5

- WHAT IS SOCIAL ANXIETY? 5
- WHY DO SO MANY STRUGGLE WITH IT? 6
- WHAT ARE THE BIGGEST ISSUES FOR THOSE WHO LACK CONFIDENCE? 6
- HOW CAN THEY OVERCOME THESE ISSUES? 7
- KNOW YOUR WEAK POINTS 7
- ACKNOWLEDGE YOUR STRENGTHS 11
- CREATE SMALL TALK GOALS 13
- BECOME A BETTER LISTENER 15
- IDENTIFY THE TYPE OF CONVERSATION 19

CHAPTER 2: SOCIAL FEARS 23

- UNDERSTAND YOUR ANXIETY 23
- LOOK AT THE BIG PICTURE 28
- REHEARSE IN LOW STAKE CONVERSATIONS 30
- TALK TO YOURSELF 32
- BUILD YOUR CONFIDENCE 35

CHAPTER 3: BODY LANGUAGE 39

- RELAX YOUR BODY 39
- READ THEIR MANNERISMS 42
- MIMIC THEIR BODY LANGUAGE 45
- PREPARE THE SETTING 48

CHAPTER 4: CONVERSATION TOPICS 51

- ASK A LOT OF QUESTIONS 51
- REPHRASE WHAT THEY SAID 54
- GIVE OPEN-ENDED ANSWERS 56
- IDENTIFY INTERESTS AND DISLIKES 59

CHAPTER 5: BEFORE THE CONVERSATION 63

- DO YOUR RESEARCH 63
- KNOW WHAT TOPICS TO AVOID 66
- WARM-UP BEFORE THE CONVERSATION 69
- BE PREPARED IF IT GOES WRONG 72

CHAPTER 6: DURING THE CONVERSATION 77
- GET THEIR NAME RIGHT AWAY 77
- MAKE THEM THE CENTER OF ATTENTION..79
- ASK WHAT YOU WOULD WANT TO BE ASKED 81
- KEEP IT LIGHTHEARTED...82
- MAKE THEM FEEL GOOD...85

CHAPTER 7: AFTER THE CONVERSATION 89
- HAVE AN EXIT STRATEGY 89
- DON'T PUT TOO MUCH WEIGHT ON THE OUTCOME..92
- TAKE TIME TO DECOMPRESS 95
- MOVE ON AND PREPARE FOR THE NEXT 96

CONCLUSION 99

REFERENCES 103

Introduction

Have you ever found yourself stuck in life? Surrounded by successful people who seem to be progressing, it can be hard to know how to pull yourself out of a hole. This time came to me when I was feeling low in confidence and struggling to even be around other people. What was it that everyone else had that I just couldn't seem to get for myself?

Then suddenly, I started to realize that the people who were the most successful, at least from my perspective, were just *so social*. The coworkers I envied could walk into the boss's office with their ideas and concerns and walk out leaving with exactly what they wanted, and then some. The friends I looked up to were the ones who could mingle at the party, talking to everyone there with charisma and excitement while I sat alone, anxious and overwhelmed in the corner.

After struggling with social anxiety my entire life, I felt like I had been given an unlucky personality and that this was the way life was for me. But this realization is actually what helped me get unstuck. Once I recognized that this was the main issue for me, I stopped focusing on how frustrated I was with myself and instead started to investigate the root of these problems.

Around 12% of adults in the U.S. struggle with social anxiety; 30% say it has severely impaired their lives (National Institute of Mental Health, n.d.). This isn't a problem that only me and you have. While it might be something we struggle with more than others, it doesn't have to be a definitive thing about who we are. Like many things in life, being a good conversationalist is a skill that can be improved on. Some people are natural singers, artists, and cooks. Others have to put in a little more effort to improve these talents, and that's okay!

Conversations don't have to be so difficult to manage. They can feel like the most important thing in life at times, but with a few techniques and some practice, you will walk away from this book feeling comfortable sparking up a conversation with anyone you pass. You will learn the advantages of being good at conversing while building the confidence needed to be an expert in the subject. You will discover all of the benefits that will come into your life when you improve your conversation skills.

You might ask yourself

- How can I get better at small talk?

- How can I reduce my social anxiety so it doesn't hold me back anymore?

- What are some practical steps I can take to improve my conversation skills so I can have more genuine conversations?

These are the main issues I'm going to tackle in the book. I've gathered 31 techniques that have helped me improve my skills. From awkward elevator conversations to more serious discussions with family, I've learned how to prepare for, manage, and overcome my fears with speaking so that I can gain all of the benefits of being a skillful talker.

This book will guide you through important techniques to help transform the way you conversate for the better. Throughout the book, you will learn how to

- Simplify the process of having a conversation.

- Overcome your speaking fears and manage social anxiety.

- Improve the overall quality of the conversations you are having.

After several years of experience, I went from being afraid to order a coffee to speaking to large groups of strangers with ease. With my expertise, I will ease you into this process while making you feel like you'll be able to have the same success that I did.

Even if you have been struggling your entire life, you will be able to learn how to become good at holding conversations. Most people know how much small talk can benefit their lives, and when they are good at it, they will make stronger connections and have deeper conversations with those they interact with. The problem is that people don't know how to overcome their fears and improve their skills.

Small talk has gotten harder in recent years as more serious topics and political tensions have risen in the United States and the world. More people are depressed, isolated, and struggling, making it harder to talk about lighter things and have conversations in general (Hoge, 2022). I want to help bridge that gap to get people back into a normal routine of initiating conversations and building their relationships.

Chapter 1:

Getting Started

This chapter will cover five techniques that are necessary for the beginning steps of working through your biggest conversation issues so you can craft the best plan to create small talk goals. These are

1. Know what your weaknesses are to have a starting point for your improvement.

2. Acknowledge your strengths to create a confident mindset.

3. Create small talk goals that will help you to stay on track.

4. Improve your listening skills to make conversations more natural.

5. Identify and familiarize yourself with conversation styles to adapt easily.

Before getting started, it's helpful to ensure you understand some of the answers to frequently asked questions about why someone might struggle with conversing in the first place.

What Is Social Anxiety?

Everyone feels anxious from time to time, but those who struggle with social anxiety have emotions that are too difficult to manage and can impair their ability to interact with others. While most people feel nervous on a first date, those with social anxiety might avoid dating altogether, and instead isolate. Repetition of these responses can lead to depression when consistently avoiding and isolating (Mayo Clinic, 2021). Even if you don't have social anxiety, you can still benefit from learning how to navigate your conversations. Though it's not a cure-all, being prepared will alleviate some feelings of nervousness, and over time there will be strong improvements in how someone is able to manage their anxiety.

Why Do So Many Struggle With It?

Social anxiety can be a learned behavior from parents and peers (Guest Author for rtor.org, 2020). It can also be a trait passed down genetically, as it could be the result of a specific brain structure. Generalized anxiety is the result of a fear response, which most people have. Bullying and cyberbullying have also increased in recent years, so when feelings of anxiety start in, childhood they can be more difficult to manage over time (Guest Author for rtor.org, 2020).

What Are the Biggest Issues for Those Who Lack Confidence?

The biggest issues are the feelings of nervousness. They can cause mental rumination, fear, and panic. Unmanaged anxiety can even lead to physical symptoms, like digestive issues, headaches, and shortness of breath (Florida Behavioral Health, 2019). Fearing small talk and other conversations can cause those who are struggling to avoid conversations, preventing us from having discussions that are very important for the advancement of our lives and goals.

How Can They Overcome These Issues?

These issues can be overcome by managing fear, practicing, and being prepared for the conversations. Each social interaction is a learning experience and a reminder of how common these talks can be. Practicing normalizes conversing so that it doesn't feel like a big, scary event each time. Frequent practice and preparation create the sense that having a discussion is an everyday occurrence like brushing your teeth or working out rather than a stress-inducing event. When conversing is more routine, it becomes easier each time, but first it requires understanding those obstacles:

- fear over the outcome

- anxiety about messing up

- stress after the conversation

In addition, it's important to know why they are there in the first place. This can start by recognizing insecurities to strengthen areas of talking that might be weak.

Know Your Weak Points

What are your biggest insecurities? Do you clam up? Do you talk too much?

Knowing these will lay the groundwork for what to focus on when practicing how to conversate.

Everyone has something that they want to work on. Knowing your weak points provides a good starting point for improvement. In identifying your weak points, you may realize you have specific feelings about yourself which could, in turn, feed into these weaknesses. For example, if you're creating a list of your weaknesses and you write down that you don't like your hair, your style, and even certain facial features, that shows a pattern of appearance-related judgments against yourself. You then might realize you blame yourself for your unhappiness, creating a cycle of self-confidence issues. In reality, a lot of these insecurities have likely been presented to you from society, parents, and peers.

If you think everything about yourself is terrible, that's also a sign that in general, your confidence is very low. Pay attention to what these weaknesses are, and list them out. Get a journal or open a new document on your computer and start typing the things that you think you struggle with the most. Some people might begin with their level of nervousness. Being afraid of what to bring up when it comes time to talk can be difficult. Being put on the spot or getting asked questions that you aren't sure of what the answer is can also make it more difficult to think on your feet. Potentially being confronted with these situations is enough to discourage people from seeking out conversations in the first place.

Other people might struggle because they are the opposite. Perhaps they talk way too much. If you are constantly going on about a subject that somebody else might not even be that interested in, it can be hard to know when to cut the conversation off. When over explaining yourself, you might find that you're revealing unnecessary information, making yourself feel more vulnerable and insecure. Oversharing usually isn't as big of a deal as we might think it is. However, struggling with that and wanting to limit how much you share is a perfectly fine goal to have. Oversharing and talking too much can lead to more anxious thoughts and rumination. Rumination is the repetition of certain negative thoughts. The repetitive nature of these thoughts makes them feel even worse, adding more emotional weight to them.

When you have the basis for what these weak points are, it will be a lot easier for you to focus on specific areas of improvement. When you have a direct idea of how to improve in your mind, then you can manage your skills as you go and better recognize whether or not you are improving.

There's an important distinction to remember between self-reflection and self-hate. Being able to reflect on yourself means that you're looking at actionable things that you can improve on. Self-hatred can often lead to the creation of an inner bully. For example, if you are a guitar player, your guitar instructor might tell you that you need to work on some of your finger work if you want to be a better player. A bully would tell you that you are really bad at playing guitar and you should just give up while you're ahead of the game.

Knowing your weak points means building your inner constructive critic while silencing your inner bully. This is the first step towards acknowledging the way that you speak to yourself. For the most part, you're likely insecure and struggling because you are your own biggest critic.

Constructive criticism is what you want to aim for. Of course, there are probably people who might have told you things in the past that made you feel insecure:

- You talk too much.
- What's the point?
- You're terrible at holding conversations!

These kinds of things might have been mentioned in the past, but most of your biggest insecurities are likely accelerated by your own thoughts and anxieties.

Self-reflection increases the amount that you're able to understand about who you are. The reason we are harder on ourselves than others is because we don't get to know ourselves in the same way that another person might.

You know your thoughts, and sometimes those can be really messy. Who you truly are is a combination of your actions and the things that you share with other people. Identifying these core values, what your beliefs are, and what you bring to the picture gives you a greater sense of the amazing and wonderful person you are. Being so self-critical and struggling with social anxiety often causes us to tip the scale in a negative way. The more you get to know yourself, the more you'll end up liking yourself because it's a balancing of the scales.

Self-doubt is as common as being hypercritical. However, just because it is normal to have these things in your life doesn't mean it will facilitate a successful life. Self-reflection helps you dive deeper into your own perspective, so that you can shift things in a neutral way. Not only will this be temporarily helpful in boosting your confidence, but in improving it long-term, too. You're still going to make some mistakes, and there will be moments that you might feel like you botched the conversation. You might have anxious feelings and ruminate after certain conversations. However, by practicing self-reflection, you'll be able to get to the root of what is going on and why you're feeling that way.

For example, if you keep beating yourself up because you feel like you talk too much during lunch with your friend, you might tell yourself, "I really hate myself. Nobody wants to listen to what I have to say. I need to learn to just shut up." These thoughts are really mean and not productive in any way. Instead, dive deeper and figure out what it is that you're actually trying to tell yourself when you're being hypercritical.

Maybe you feel like you overshared and now you're feeling extremely vulnerable. Perhaps you didn't get the reaction that you might have needed or wanted from the other person, making you feel as though you were not sharing valuable information with them. Instead of telling yourself something very harsh like, "You need to learn to shut up," instead you can use this as a way to reflect when you are having conversations with other people to monitor and pull back a little bit as to what you're sharing to give them an opportunity to talk as well.

When you are beating yourself up, you're going to go from extreme to extreme in these types of conversations. In the first one, you talked too much because you were anxious and trying to work through your thoughts; and then in the next conversation, you completely withdraw and don't share anything at all. Both of these conversations aren't going to help you improve. What will set you up for success is recognizing what those weaknesses and insecurities can really tell you about yourself. It is then that you'll be able to avoid these pitfalls in the next conversation.

It's also important to wade through those identified weaknesses to determine where they came from. Getting to the root of these problems will make it easier for you to determine whether or not they're true statements or just things that you've been led to believe through repetition.

For example, if you had critical parents who constantly picked on the things that you said or made you afraid to share what was on your mind, that's going to lead to a lot more insecurities compared to someone who was encouraged to share their feelings and express themselves however they might have wanted.

Having bullies who were always picking on you and making you feel belittled and stupid while you were in school might make you afraid to share. Instead, it may have created the desire to hold back. Your mind and body are trying to protect itself from these traumatic experiences, so you might withdraw to avoid living through the pain of being bullied. Once you can reflect on this and have a better grasp of why the insecurities are there, it will be easier to know how to remove them from your life.

Acknowledge Your Strengths

Now that you know that you have to understand your weaknesses, it's time to smooth over some of the tender wounds of self-reflection to acknowledge your strengths. It's not easy to overcome some of the things that make us afraid to be who we are, but you should feel proud of yourself already for making the decision to self-improve. If you can replace negative feelings by acknowledging your strengths, it becomes so much easier to feel confident and boost yourself up in the times that you really need it.

Start by looking at the things that friends point out as your beneficial qualities. What are you known for? Some friends might tell you that you're an amazing listener. Other friends might think you're hilarious and say that you're the funniest person they've ever met. Some people might tell you that you're a colorful storyteller and that you're filled with fun facts. There are strengths that you already have, even when it doesn't feel like it. You have to know how to sift through some of those damaging thoughts to pull out your strengths. What unique aspects of your personality can you develop and play into so that you feel more confident when talking to other people?

Funny people might be good at poking fun of themselves and coming up with jokes. If you are a good listener, maybe focus more on asking questions and hearing the other person out.

When you can forgive yourself for past mistakes, you'll stop beating yourself up so much. We can build resentment towards ourselves. Just as you might be passive aggressive to somebody who really bothers you, you can act with the same kind of aggression towards yourself. If you forgive yourself and move on from these past mistakes, you can instead focus on the future, which is something that you actually have control over.

When you point out your own strengths and the other benefits in your life, such as being a good friend, a good parent, or a good coworker, then you have legitimate backup to your claims when managing self-criticism.

If you tell yourself, "I'm a loser, nobody likes me," you can remind yourself, "Well I do have an amazing group of friends who enjoy hanging out with me. I am not a loser because I am a productive member of my community, and I'm an active participant in my job. I am not alone because I have so many family members around me who really care about my well-being."

You do have strengths somewhere deep down even if you're suppressing them. You can bring them out. You have to do this by being easier on yourself and taking care of yourself. Dive deep into who you are and discover your personality. What comes easy to you that might be difficult for others? What would you do if the world ended tomorrow? If you had to evacuate your house, what three things would you grab?

Using questions like these to engage in deep self-reflection gives you a better understanding of who you are as a person, making it easier to develop a healthy relationship with yourself.

Create Small Talk Goals

Creating goals will help to lay out the milestones you want to achieve while practicing small talk. Having things to work towards and specific things to do will keep you on track so that you continue to nourish your conversation skills.

Solid goal creation starts when you identify why it's important to you to have goals in the first place. Why do you want to be better at small talk? Do you want to advance in your career? Do you want to stop feeling so bad about yourself after social interactions?

Do you want to go out in public more? Do you feel lonely at home and struggle to make friends? There's a reason why you're here. Creating appropriate goals starts by identifying those reasons.

Acknowledging the importance of adding goals to your lifestyle will give you more motivation to maintain the habits needed to reach them.

There are important rules to goal setting that you should consider. A good way to remember these rules is by understanding the SMART goal system. This is an acronym that stands for specific, measurable, attainable, relevant, and timed goals.

Goals should be specific to yourself. Wanting to be better at talking in general is a good starting point. Take it a step further to create more specific goals based around the most important factors in your life. Are you struggling at work the most? Is it your social life that you're suffering with? If you don't have an understanding of the specific milestones you want to achieve, it'll be harder to stay on track. Self-improvement is all about taking initiative and responsibility for your own well-being, so if you follow a generic guideline, you won't have that motivation to force yourself to do things outside of your comfort zone.

Being a better speaker is all about pushing yourself past the boundaries you've created. Now it's time to stay motivated and work through your issues so that you can achieve your specific goals.

Goals should also be measurable. When it comes to something like talking, it's a little bit harder to notice progress. A goal like wanting to read 100 books in a year is easier to measure because you can keep track of the number of books you read. Deciding what measurable attributes to assign to your goals will determine your timeline and the actionable steps to achieve these goals. This is why having a specific goal is important because you can break it down into little milestones.

Goals need to be attainable. Wanting to become a public speaker in a week's time might be difficult because you need to establish connections and gain authoritative experience for people who want to hire you as a public speaker. A goal like scheduling a doctor's appointment or landing a job interview within a week's time is a little more realistic.

Being good at talking is important, but there's a lot more that goes behind the scenes of wanting to be a public speaker. You also have to realize that improvement is nonlinear. Even though you feel really confident one day doesn't mean that you're going to have those same emotions the next day. Wanting to perform a stand-up comedy set by the end of the week when you have never done so before might be a little bit unrealistic. You need to give yourself more warm-up time to really achieve that goal.

When you're setting goals that are unattainable, what ends up happening is that you fail to reach these milestones, therefore feeling even worse about yourself. Instead of your small successes pushing you forward, your small failures end up setting you back.

Your goals should be relevant to who you are and the things that you desire to add to your life. Don't set goals just because somebody else has these goals. For example, if you dislike children, setting a goal for having five kids isn't relevant to you. Though it might feel like it's a milestone that you *should* achieve in your life, it still needs to be something that you're passionate about or else you're always going to push it off.

Finally, your goals need to be timed. This is another motivating factor to help push you forward. If you don't have a goal that is timed, you might never really put the energy into trying to achieve it.

Some examples of goals might be to go out in public more, reduce rumination after social interactions, or maybe to become a professional speaker or a person in a communications position.

Other small talk goals might include:

- Participating in habits like singing when other people are around.
- Socializing and making more friends.
- Establishing your boundaries and becoming more assertive.
- Sharing information about yourself with others.
- Decreasing social blunders and reducing anxiety after these interactions.

Take a moment to write out your small talk goals and a potential timeframe for reaching them. After that, create small milestones that will help keep you in line with achieving these things.

Become a Better Listener

Knowing how to talk means knowing how to listen. Paying attention to the other person allows you to keep the conversation flowing while building trust in the other person.

What are some things that other people have done that made you feel invalidated, or like they weren't listening to you?

Did they walk away mid conversation? Were they texting on their phone while they listened to you? Were they looking around or even talking to other people while you were trying to talk? What are the things that have made you feel worse about yourself?

Now, the hard question to ask is whether or not *you* have done these things to somebody else. Sometimes it might not feel like we're being intentionally bad listeners, but the things that we're doing can make it appear that way.

If somebody was not listening to you when you were talking, it doesn't mean that they disliked what you had to say. Perhaps they were hosting the party and were looking around because they were nervous about everybody having a good time. Maybe there is an emergency going on that they were trying to communicate with someone about, while still trying to put the effort in to give you attention, even if it was half attention.

Of course, some people are bad listeners. You'll run into plenty of people in your lifetime who would much rather talk about themselves than hear anything anybody else has to say. At the same time, we have to recognize that actions don't always reflect our intentions. If you are texting while somebody else is talking, even though you're listening to them, it can still come off rude.

Having a good conversation requires two parties. Even when you're speaking on your own, there's still a listener, whether it's yourself or the notes that you're dictating. Having somebody who is fully engaged in the conversation is required to make it go smoothly. To lead these conversations and be somebody that others admire for the way that they talk means improving your listening skills, no matter where they might be at right now.

One of the worst things that you can do is plan out what you want to say next, instead of actually hearing what the other person is saying. This is especially true in conflicts. If you're fighting with your spouse, and they're sharing why they're upset, they might be further flustered if you're trying to plan your defense rather than listening to what they're saying. What's required is hearing them out even if it takes you a couple of seconds to respond. That's better than ignoring what they have to say, furthering the conflict even more.

Summarizing the other person's conversation and speaking it back to them can be good or bad. This is something that you're going to have to gauge on your own when participating in discussions. If it's a serious conversation in which somebody's sharing their feelings, it might be tricky territory to summarize what they're saying because you don't want to miss the point.

If one of your employees comes into your office and starts sharing with you that they're feeling stressed and overwhelmed and you say, "Alright, so do you want me to cut your hours?" that might be completely missing the point and could sound threatening to the employee. Maybe they just need some extra assistance, so listen to what they have to say. If your spouse tells you that they're feeling neglected and that you're not pulling your weight in the relationship, you might say "Oh, so you think I'm just a bad spouse?" Sometimes summarizing things can completely miss the point and make the situation worse.

However, summarizing new information is a good way to show that you are listening to the other person. If you're at a job interview and they tell you that one of your main job requirements is going to be delegating tasks and assigning different projects to various people, you can summarize that by saying, "So, I'm going to be a team leader?" That's a good way to show that you comprehend the information.

Other great listening techniques are to use small, encouraging phrases as others are talking to signify your engagement with the conversation. This also keeps you focused so that instead of planning things you want to say in your mind, you're listening to them and helping push the conversation along. These would be little phrases like, "mhm, uh-huh," or "I understand where you're coming from." When you give these validating responses, the other person is likely to share a lot more with you rather than if you were staring at them, stone-faced with no reply.

Ask questions about how the other person is feeling to help clarify the situation. Going back to the example about the employee coming into your office, you might say, "I understand. It seems like you might be feeling burned out or overwhelmed?" They could still respond that they disagree or that you got the assessment wrong, but at least it won't be inaccurately summarizing or trying to wrap up the conversation.

Try to remember that not everybody wants advice. Sometimes people only want to complain and get their feelings out. You might not understand what your feelings mean until you're actually sharing them and turning them into words.

It's important to ask somebody whether or not they want advice, or if they only want you to listen. For example, if a friend starts complaining that her partner doesn't take her on dates enough, or that they're too controlling and jealous, your first thought might be to say "Well, you need to set some boundaries."

Not only can it be frustrating to that person because they don't want the advice, but it might almost be invalidating and could come off like you're trying to diminishingly summarize the problem and quickly move past it. In reality, they might be looking for support or validation for having these feelings. A lot of times people already know the steps that they need to take to solve their problems; however, from you, they want encouragement to know that they're making the right decision.

In this situation you might say instead, "Oh, wow, I'm sorry you're dealing with that. I would be frustrated, too. Have you talked to your partner about this?"

Then the friend can share, "Yes, I have. But they don't seem to listen, I don't know what to do, and I really need help."

Get consent to share advice instead of putting your friend into a position to have to say something like, "Yes, I have. I'll figure it out. I'm sorry. I just want to rant. I need to get this off my chest." Then you will know the purpose of the conversation and that she really just wants support and encouragement from a friend right now. Sometimes listening means understanding what the type of conversation is so that you can react appropriately.

Identify the Type of Conversation

Different conversations call for different reactions and strategies, so being able to identify the situation you're in will make it easier to act accordingly. Is it a serious meeting? Is it a short chat?

The majority of conversations are likely going to be casual. You probably talk to a few friends a day or maybe you go home and have a conversation with your family every night.

Other people might have more professional conversations than casual ones. You might talk to your coworkers more than anybody at home, maybe because you live alone or don't have many friends that you hang out with. Regardless, it's important to understand these types of conversations so that you can follow a few of the unspoken guidelines that usually come along with them.

You can remember the types of conversations by remembering the five Ds. These are

- dictating
- debate
- discussion
- deliberation
- dialogue

Dictating is frequently involved in power situations. This is when you are giving directions and instructions to other people. This will be the delegation type of conversation.

This is a conversation that you have between yourself and a person that you want to complete a task. A boss dictates to their employee that they want them to manage certain projects. A parent dictates to their child that they want them to clean up their bedroom.

When dictating conversations, one of the most important things is to be firm and clear. You can never assume that the other person already knows what you want to share with them. You can't expect people to read your mind. The clearer you are with the instructions, the less chance there is of a conflict occurring.

The other aspect of dictating conversations is that they require some sensitivity. If you are dictating to your child or your employee in an aggressive tone and showing frustration, that is going to change how they end up completing that task. Though they might still follow through, they could be nervous and anxious the whole time, causing them to not perform to the best of their ability. Being aggressive can change the dynamic of a dictating conversation. Somebody is more likely to mess up on tasks when they are feeling nervous because they are also afraid. It can cause the person to become distracted and focused on wondering why you're upset with them. This is especially true for how a child might react if a parent is aggressive towards them. Being sensitive in how you dictate can really change the dynamic of the conversation.

The second D is debate. These conversations have little to no power imbalance, instead there's a more structured argument. We often associate arguing with aggression and anger but that's not always the case.

You might have a debate with your boss. Perhaps they're blaming you for messing up a recent sales order. You might debate with them because you're trying to share your perspective to have them better understand where you're coming from and why that mistake was made in the first place.

Debating has a lot of the same rules as dictating. The main difference is that usually the goal in a debate is for both people to share their sides, which may or may not be opposing, and hopefully result in an outcome in which the other person gains a new perspective.

With both dictating and debating, the person who is the target of the aggression also has to remember a few things about managing the other person. If your boss is screaming at you and being rude, you deserve to stand up for yourself. If a customer comes in, the power imbalance can feel different, but if they are screaming at you and telling you what to do, you can still take a moment to say, "I don't like the way you're talking to me."

You might tell somebody, "The way you're speaking is making me feel belittled." You can share your concerns about how the other person is treating you by focusing on your own feelings. While we can't control the emotions of others, we can properly express our own feelings which can potentially alter the response of the other person.

The third kind of conversation is discussion. Discussions involve open conversations in which two people are sharing thoughts and ideas with each other. There's usually not a formal goal in these conversations. In a debate, you already have your beliefs, and you want the other person to understand them; but in a discussion, you might be open to changing your mind. You may not be trying to change the other person's mind and are sharing how you feel. A discussion is usually an exchange of facts in conversations. Discussions really don't have many guidelines other than that they should still be civil.

If you do notice that the other person is seemingly feeling defensive or starting to get aggressive, it's okay to pull back. Not every debate needs to be won; they might have something else going on or some deeper issues that they need to work through on their own if they're taking extreme offense to what you're saying in a casual discussion.

When you're having discussions with people in a professional setting, it's important to avoid certain topics (which we will cover in a later chapter).

The fourth kind of conversation is deliberation. This is when two people are coming together to make a decision that will benefit both parties. It differs from a debate because, typically, the goals of the two people in a debate are different, but in a deliberation, the goals are the same. An example of this situation would be you and a coworker figuring out the best way to manage an issue at work, or it could be a deliberation on which house to purchase with your spouse, or what school to send your child to. Deliberations are important because if you're not careful, they could turn into a debate quickly. Deliberations require that before the decision is made, both of you have to decide the ideal outcome. If you're deciding what school to pick for your child, you and your spouse might have different ideas of what would be the best based on location, size, and academic achievements of past students. What you both agree on is that you are having the deliberation to choose the best school possible.

If you notice that the other person is trying to turn it into a debate, you can pull back and have a moment of reflection to reestablish the beneficial mutual outcome.

The fifth D is dialogue. This is exploring the other person, their thoughts, and their perspectives. It can be talking honestly and openly. It's creating a safe space for you to share some of those deeper feelings.

Dialogue is different from discussion in that it's usually more serious, and there is a goal of presenting new and more detailed information. A discussion might involve a topic like a recent movie they watched. A dialogue might be exploring feminism within modern filmmaking. It's taking a discussion one level deeper.

Once you identify these types of conversations, you'll understand them better as you're participating in them. It can make it easier to manage things as conflicts begin to arise. We'll be referencing some of these throughout the rest of the book, so it's good to familiarize yourself with the various types of conversations.

Chapter 2:

Social Fears

When weeding a garden, you have to dig deep beneath the soil to pull out the entire plant. If not, it will keep coming back. You can cover the soil and add thick mulch, but before you know it, the weed will sprout back through. Getting to the root of your biggest social anxiety setbacks will help you to dig deep and get rid of them so they don't keep popping back up. There are five important steps to overcome your social fears:

1. Understand your anxiety so you know how to resolve issues as they arise.

2. Look at the big picture to help gain perspective on the stress of conversations.

3. Rehearse in situations that aren't high stakes to practice for important talks.

4. Practice talking to yourself to feel more comfortable with speaking.

5. Build your confidence up once you manage your fears to help you succeed.

Understand Your Anxiety

What is fear? Sometimes we become so afraid of the other person that we think of them as scarier than they are. They are not the fear we create of them in our head.

Fear is common and everyone experiences it in some form. It's a response to a specific trigger. Anxiety is when fear is repeated even after the trigger might not be there and can arise when the fear is no longer real. For example, many people fear they might get into a car accident when going on a long road trip. Safety measures usually alleviate this fear, and preparing for the road trip also helps. Someone with anxiety, however, might end up never getting into a car in their life because they are constantly afraid they might get into an accident.

In relation to conversing, most people would agree that large social events, job interviews, and public speaking can cause nervousness and fear beforehand. However, someone with social anxiety might experience panic attacks before social events, never go to job interviews, struggle to find employment, or avoid talking altogether because of the excessive fear they experience.

Anxiety becomes much easier to manage once you understand the point of fear and worry in the first place. If you slip and fall, your instinct is to reach for something to hold you up. If you feel sick, it's your instinct to rest and take care of yourself. If you feel unsafe in your home, it's an instinct to lock the doors and check out the windows to make sure nobody's lurking around your property.

Fear is a signal that lets our bodies know we need to take action to keep ourselves preserved. At the end of the day, your mind and body are all focused on making sure that you stay alive. This natural self-preservation is built into all living organisms. Everybody uses defense mechanisms. Even certain plants, like roses, have defense mechanisms to keep them safe. Thorns ward off predators. You can look at the biological purposes of many aspects of living organisms to determine how they're being used as forms of self-preservation.

Humans are animals, so we have these basic preservation tactics. Everyone has a fight or flight instinct that helps them to respond to a potential threat. When fear is presented, you might confront this fear or flee. Think of the way a bunny might react versus a bear. If you're walking through the woods and stumble into a bunny's territory, they will likely run away. A bear might fight you or attack. Different situations also call for different responses. If you're holding a bunny, it might still fight by biting you if it wants to get away. A bear might choose to run from a hunter or a large vehicle rather than trying to attack.

If someone is being aggressive towards you, you can either fight them back or choose instead to run away. Even if you can't physically flee, you may do things like mentally check out, use alcohol, or use mind altering substances as a way to cope; these can all act as other forms of flight. Some people might not be violent with others, but maybe they are with objects around them like punching a hole in the wall or throwing a remote at the TV.

Fear is meant to keep us safe, but when unmanaged, it can have the opposite effect. These fears and anxieties all boil down to five core fears. If you can identify each of your fears, and label them as one part of the five core fears, you can remind yourself why you are safe and that everything is going to be okay. It becomes a lot easier to manage your fears once you pick them apart to understand the core truths that these fears are trying to tell you.

The first core fear is extinction. We have a natural urge to preserve ourselves and to reproduce to continue our species.

Dying is one of the biggest and most natural fears that all of us have. Sometimes these fears are as simple as wanting to stay alive because you enjoy your life and have family and friends that you love. You probably fear death because it could be extremely painful, long, or excruciating. The fear of not knowing what happens after we die is something that keeps a lot of people awake at night.

This is a very common anxiety and a lot of social anxiety, self-esteem issues, and struggles with conversation skills can boil down to this specific fear.

If you're alone at a bar, surrounded by a bunch of strangers, you might have the natural fear that one of them may hurt you. How you talk to strangers at the bar will differ from how you might interact with a group of kindergarteners.

The second core fear is mutilation. This is the idea that you are going to lose some part of your bodily structure. Not only is this a limb like your arm or your leg, but it could be something internal like your stomach or your heart. Even if we're completely safe from mutilation, our brain doesn't eliminate the fear. It can still manifest itself in unexpected ways.

This fear of mutilation is why we are afraid of things like spiders or other animals. The risk of getting bit by something or attacked by an animal can be very scary.

This is also related to the third core fear, which is loss of autonomy. This is losing bodily control, whether you become physically restricted or trapped in some way. Control being taken away from you as a human can be very anxiety inducing. Not only do these fears manifest themselves physically, but they can become emotionally entangled as well. Choosing a dead-end job might make you feel as though you've lost some of your autonomy. Some people are afraid of having children because they don't want to lose control over their life.

The fourth core fear, separation, is the opposite of the third core fear. Separation makes us afraid that we are going to be outcast from the group, of being exiled, or chastised. For example, look at today's society: a lot of people have the fear of being socially, professionally, or interpersonally *canceled*. It's not like we send people off to an island anymore but losing your role in society and being rejected by your peers can be a terrifying experience.

Finally, this leads into the fifth core fear which is your fear of ego death. This is the fear of being humiliated, being rejected by others, and not having the approval of your peers. This might be the biggest fear you have as somebody who's struggling with social anxiety, along with the fear of separation. Often these fears can be derivative of our deepest insecurities.

If you are often dependent on other people, whether it's through their assistance or validation and approval, it will really increase your desire to please other people to get inner validation. When you break these fears down, you can start to understand how the reasons why you're so afraid of talking to other people can lead to bigger core fears like being rejected.

We are group animals, which means that we depend on other people to fulfill our needs. Think about the hunter and gatherer strategy: Hunters were dependent on gatherers for some of their food, especially if they couldn't fulfill hunting needs—and vice versa.

There were periods when humans couldn't find something to hunt, or other seasonal and weather changes meant there wasn't anything to gather, so the collaboration between the two helped to create the healthy humans we are today through a diverse diet.

Working in a group meant that some people were responsible for one job, and other people were responsible for their own tasks. They only had to focus on one task rather than worrying about completing all the tasks on their own. This kind of community was built over time and affects the way we interact with others to this day.

While no longer hunter-gatherers, we still depend on people for things that we can't provide for ourselves.

Everybody wants to have friends or be a part of a group because it feels good to go out in public, have fun, and share experiences. When it comes to your career, there's often people that you have to work with. If you're a doctor, you depend on the nurses and medical assistants to help treat patients. A doctor cannot do as much on their own. This traces all the way to the people checking in patients and working in the billing department.

If you are a parent, despite sometimes feeling like you're in this alone, you *do* have people you can depend on, whether it's the doctor to help your child when they're sick, or the teacher that educates your children. It's also the peers who fulfill the needs of your own child. You want your kid to go out, have friends, and be a part of a group.

Our brains seek out and want to protect these desires. Fear is the background noise that reminds us to make the best decisions for ourselves. For example, you might think it's fun to go swimming in a secluded spot you found deep in the forest. However, your fear is going to tell you to look for snakes or leeches in the water, or spiders hanging from the trees. Your fear is useful because it helps protect you. It makes you second guess your decisions to ensure that you're acting in the safest manner. Unfortunately, these fears can also become too much for us to handle to the point that they hold us back.

If you are going to the swimming hole, it's good to be aware and notice potential threats, but allowing these fears to be in control and prevent you from going can be very damaging to your life.

Breaking these fears down to determine why they are there and what they are trying to tell you will give the control back to you rather than letting anxieties take power over your life.

Look at the Big Picture

It can be difficult to not let these fears overpower you. One little thought can spiral all the way back to the deepest insecurities in your mind. One minute, you might catch a little attitude coming from the cashier at the gas station. Next, you're sitting in your car thinking back to your childhood and feeling like a 6-year-old getting scolded by their parents. One of the best ways to gain control over these fears is to look at the big picture.

It's easy to get stuck in our head and think of the what-ifs. Sure, one conversation could change everything. Sharing ideas with the right person or bringing your concerns to someone who can make a difference could result in something life-changing for you. All of a sudden, you might freak out about making sure you greet them in the right way or say all the perfect things. But in reality, if this conversation is that important, it will likely end up that way anyway without you having to worry about the teeniest little details.

Perspective can shape everything. Have you ever been attacked by a wasp or bee, panicking because you couldn't see the bug? Now think back to a time when you saw someone else under attack. It was likely a lot easier for you to maintain your composure and stay collected because you had eyes on the insect. You had a clearer picture of the situation, giving you the necessary perspective to understand that everything is fine.

This is the kind of mentality to have during a conversation. It can seem like your words are the end-all of a major situation, but in reality, the other person is likely thinking the same of themself. You're not coming off the way that you think you are. They don't know the thoughts in your head because they are having their own thoughts, which is distracting them from some of your cues you might be giving.

The other person you're conversing with is likely just as nervous as you, if not more so! Sharing these anxieties can help break the ice as well as give you a more comfortable position. For example, if you're talking to a friend or going on a date, you can share with the other person that you're feeling a little nervous. Sure, it might be awkward, but they might share that they're nervous too, cutting some of the tension in the conversation.

One conversation is a small moment in time, and there will be plenty more. It's hard to not let every conversation be a definitive moment in your life, but remember that you likely only assign this importance to negative conversations. There have probably been plenty of great discussions you had that you don't remember, but the most embarrassing chat from a decade ago might still haunt your thoughts from time to time. It's important to recognize that these feelings are normal, but they don't have to rule your life.

You probably don't remember a lot of conversations you've had. I would almost guarantee there is someone out there in the world, anxious over a conversation they had with you that you don't even remember. The small embarrassing things that you've been clinging to are likely to never cross the other person's mind. Even if they do remember some of your social blunders, they likely don't put as much weight on it as you do.

Ask yourself: Do you think of other people's mistakes as often as your own? Do you think others focus on your mistakes more so than their own? When we free ourselves from the fear of making mistakes, it is a lot easier to be yourself in conversations and let go of the anxiety that normally holds you back.

Rehearse in Low Stake Conversations

There are many people in the world and a lot of them want to talk to you, even though it might not feel that way. There are plenty of people who enjoy having conversations and getting to know new people.

The best way to make you more comfortable talking is through practice. Practicing is important because that's how we troubleshoot our issues, while also being comfortable with negative outcomes in situations that are a lower stakes. If you have a horribly awkward interaction with somebody at the grocery store, you can move on and be fine. If you have a horrible interaction with a friend that you really admire and want to impress, that might be something that bothers you over time and feeds those fears, which, in turn, holds you back more.

Having small conversations will give you practice. For example, if you only talk to two people a week, you're going to put a lot of weight on those two conversations. If you talk to two people a day, by the end of the week, you have had almost 20 conversations and can tell yourself only one of fourteen of these discussions were awkward. That will give you the encouragement and reminder that conversations aren't so scary.

Practicing conversation skills can happen anywhere—from your job, to when you're walking down the street. It's important to not always expect an engaging conversation from the other person and to remember you can't force them to interact. Somebody that you're trying to talk to might have worse anxiety than you and you might not know it. It's not like we wear a badge with the level of anxiety we have on our shirts all the time. They might also be busy or distracted, like if you're trying to strike up a conversation with a barista during rush hour. If you talk to someone on the train during your commute, they might give you a weird look and go back to reading or staring out the window. Though it might be uncomfortable, it still helps you to get used to the idea that the conversation might not always go smoothly.

In fact, getting rejected by some people will be helpful. You can live through that experience you fear so much and realize it's really not that bad at the end of the day. After a month or two you're going to forget about that person who was a little rude to you in the grocery store or somebody that gave you a weird look when you tried to strike up a conversation.

At the end of the day, this form of practice is going to make you feel more confident in yourself. This will allow you to build a trusting relationship with yourself, honing in on interpersonal skills that will allow you to succeed in life.

You will feel more prepared for these conversations in the future while realizing it's not that big of a deal if a conversation turns a little sour.

Start practicing at your job. Do you have coworkers? Strike up conversations with these people. It's so easy to go about your day, never really talk to anybody, and get your tasks done.

Not only does talking with coworkers help build relationships, but it can make the day go by a little faster as well. If you are looking for a job, starting in a retail or customer service position might help you practice some of these conversation skills. When you're a cashier at a retail store or a server, you are forced to talk to people. You can't go through these jobs being silent the entire time.

Bartending and customer service jobs over the phone give you the ability to hear your voice out loud and interact with people in a professional way. There's no personal pressure to share deep information. These kinds of conversations can be very surface level and focused on small talk.

You can talk about the weather. Maybe you talk about a new episode of a show you watched last night. Perhaps you ask them what their plans for the weekend are. You can ask about small things and have low stakes conversations to get you used to interacting with other people.

If you have a position in which you're working from home and you don't really talk to other people, that doesn't mean you can't still practice. There are many other volunteer positions that could help you with this.

Nursing homes and senior centers are places where visitors are very much welcome. You can start talking to people, hear their experiences, and not only learn something interesting about the other person, but practice in a way that really isn't that big of a deal. If you go into a senior living community and find how you can be a volunteer, you'll discover that a lot of people really just want someone to talk to; they don't care if you're the best person ever at having a conversation. They aren't going to mind if you're a little awkward. They just want some company and some stimulation.

You can also interact through fundraising or canvassing. If you have a certain political party that you're passionate about, getting the word out and canvassing from door to door is one of the greatest ways that you can really throw yourself into these situations that are going to force you out of your comfort zone. It might be awkward at first, but it's a great way to really deal with that intense rejection. People might slam the door in your face, or they might get into a fight with you because they hold views of a different political party.

You can take these conversations online to practice. Many communities on social media sites like Reddit can provide opportunities for you to share your thoughts, opinions, and hear those of others. This makes it even easier to get your voice out there because you don't have to actually do the talking. You never come face to face with another person, and you don't have to worry about getting judged or rejected. In fact, you can delete your entire account if things go really wrong.

Of course, once you start chatting with people online, there are a lot of safety measures to keep in mind. Make sure that you are going about things in a smart way; nonetheless, it's a reminder that there are so many opportunities for you to talk in all avenues of the world.

Talk to Yourself

A common horror movie trope is the image of the unhinged villain talking to themselves in the mirror. While it can make a creepy visual, in reality, talking to yourself can be beneficial to your health. We talk to ourselves all day long in our mind, so why not allow those words to come out? How uncomfortable you are with the sound of your voice is proof that you should likely warm up to it.

Hearing your own voice can sometimes feel wrong and awkward. We get so used to the way it sounds in our head, the real echo of our voice can be jarring. It starts a spiral of thoughts: Is this how I always sound? Is my voice annoying? Do other people think these things? Before you know it, you're avoiding talking altogether to ensure you're never confronted with the sound of your own voice. By practicing self-talk out loud, you enable your mind to feel relaxed by your voice rather than afraid. Whether you're chatting with a friend or recording a speech that will be made into a video, frequent self-talk practice boosts your confidence, giving you the courage to lead these conversations.

Talking to yourself out loud helps you become less distracted, making it easier to focus. Have you ever noticed that you easily burn through a task when you're talking? Chatting on the phone on your way to work or striking up a conversation with a customer while at work can make the day go by quicker. If you narrate the tasks you're doing, it can make you feel more assured by your actions and less focused on the negative self-talk that can make us second-guess ourselves.

Practice talking in the mirror—you may pick up on things you didn't realize you were doing. Some people frown more often than they think, or maybe the smiles and head nods are too aggressive. Limit how much you do this at first. It could be more helpful to practice taking selfies first if you feel uncomfortable being in front of the mirror too long.

Talking out loud to yourself while doing small tasks can make you more comfortable with your voice. This could be small things like going through a checklist or even singing while you clean.

Sometimes just hearing your own voice out loud can help it be less jarring. As you become more comfortable with the sound of your voice while carrying out these tasks, you might try adding in the use of recording devices. If you're practicing for a big speech or are struggling in job interviews, it might be beneficial to listen to the way you talk and use your body. This will give you a better sense of how you come off to others. There could be things you're doing that are easily fixable, but are holding you back. Sometimes anxiety can come off as anger or judgment. The things we're feeling can come out through our facial expressions while talking, and other people can easily pick up on this.

When you are really struggling, affirmations can help. These are repetitive phrases that can condition your mind into believing and achieving something through visualization. When a desire becomes a focal point and reality that your mind is comfortable with, you'll be more likely to seek it out in your day-to-day activities.

Self-talk can also help you reduce the negative limitations you might be unknowingly imposing on yourself. For example, saying something like, "I'm not good enough," out loud can give you a new perspective on how much negative self-talk you allow into your life. Hearing the mean things you say with your own voice can be hard to do because we feel the negative emotions that come along with them more intensely. By practicing reducing negative self-talk, we give ourselves the ability to manage these sayings and turn them into encouraging things instead. Consider the examples below of how to turn negative self-talk into positive self-talk:

- *I'm not good enough.*/ **I am improving the things I don't like about myself.**

- *I hate myself.*/ **I am passionate about improving.**

- *I can't do this.*/ **I know my limits and push myself to achieve my goals.**

- *Everything is terrible.*/ **I am grateful for the positive things in my life.**

- *I have nothing to look forward to.*/ **I seek out positive experiences for myself.**

Talking to yourself out loud can be comforting in times of high stress. You're going to be your main friend over the years; you can't change some things about who you are, but you can control the things you say and how you act on them. If you learn to be your biggest self-supporter, you'll increase your confidence, making you more certain of your choices. When you're panicked or struggling in a social situation, you can repeat positive affirmations to yourself in a soothing voice. A simple, "I can do this," can center you back in the moment and allow you to reconnect with yourself.

Make self-talk sound more natural for public speaking. Often when we talk out loud it can feel like a performance. You likely know the sound of someone's voice when they are stiff and rehearsed, reading line for line from a script. This gives you more practice with on-the-spot speaking, so transitioning between topics will sound more natural during speeches.

Self-talk is scientifically proven to be better for you as it helps you sort through feelings (Zoppi, 2021). It causes a moment of reflection. If you're struggling to talk to yourself comfortably, you can start in smaller ways first. This might include

- Journaling every day to begin reflecting on your emotions.
- Singing in the car or shower when you are alone.
- Write yourself a letter, whether it's your past or future self.
- Hanging out in front of a mirror.

Build Your Confidence

Outward confidence starts with inner confidence. Managing small insecurities will make you less likely to focus on them when talking with other people. If you're having a bad hair day and it gets you down, it can distract you during conversations that aren't related to hair or appearance. Walking by a mirror when you're feeling self-conscious could cause you to become distracted, leading to a desire to isolate at a social event rather than engage with others.

Below are signs that you might be struggling with self-confidence:

- Acting based on the fear of judgment from others.

- Avoiding new opportunities from fear of risk.

- Disregarding your own mistakes, not taking accountability, and blaming others for your actions and choices.

- Feeling uncomfortable when compliments are given.

- Focused on the insecurities and weaknesses you feel you have.

You can exude more confidence by following the steps below:

1. Show more enthusiasm. Even if you're unsure of yourself or the situation, exuding confidence is possible by showing excitement for the things you're involved in. This can help you set the tone of the event or conversation. If you're showing insecurity and lacking enthusiasm, it can make the other person disinterested as well.

2. Increase the energy in yourself. Speak up, increase the volume of your voice, and be clear with what you're sharing. You can lose the other party if you're too casual and not giving enough energy to a discussion. It can come off poorly to the other person, and they might end up giving you less energy back.

3. Speak up and stick with short sentences to make it easier to speak at a high volume. If your voice is shaky or you're struggling with your words, it might cause the other person to lose interest. Being nervous can be inevitable, but laughing off your mistakes can break the tension. Take a moment to smile, clear your throat, and start again. Even if you mess up again, others will be forgiving because they'll see the effort and confidence you're pushing forward.

4. Stop comparing yourself. You'll always see yourself in a negative light if you compare your weaknesses to someone else's strengths. It can feel impossible to not make unfair comparisons, especially in a world with so many different perspectives online. However, giving too much energy to your weaknesses will keep you in a cycle of low confidence.

Don't be afraid to admit you don't know it all! The fear of looking stupid or less than perfect can be debilitating. It's why procrastination can be so difficult to manage; it's easier to avoid failure if you never try at all. Everyone who is an expert has learned from their mistakes. These mistakes are the ones that you're afraid of. Push past this fear and remember that a mistake is a lesson learned for improvement in the future.

Reflect on your biggest insecurities. Where do you feel you need to improve the most? Sometimes appearance is one issue, but beyond that, our self-perception can cause deep insecurities. Your job, possessions, or status in life might make you feel less than. How can you work through these insecurities so that they don't take away from your confidence anymore?

Change negative habits to see positive changes in your life. What do you do that makes you feel bad about yourself? Small actions throughout the day can give you a big confidence boost. For example, sleeping late could lead to procrastinating work. Falling behind could lead to avoidance, and then you panic and stay up late trying to rush through tasks. This isn't successful, and so the cycle repeats.

One small choice can lead to a change in how you see yourself, so reflect on your confidence and its relation to your self-perception.

Chapter 3:

Body Language

Listening to others is a skill that extends beyond just hearing the words that come from their mouth. Noticing the smallest movements in someone's physical language and eye movement can help you better understand the things they are telling you, as well as the feelings they can't even communicate themselves. Reading body language is accomplished through four important steps:

1. Relax your body so you can pay attention to what unspoken language others see.

2. Familiarize yourself with common body language techniques to understand how to best utilize them.

3. Mimicking other people's body language can help to make everyone more comfortable.

4. Set the scene for the conversation to assist it in moving as smoothly as possible.

Relax Your Body

Our bodies convey massive, visible signals for the invisible things passing through our much smaller brains. Think of all the automatic things you do every day. Scratching your head, adjusting positions in your bed, and tying your shoe are all things we do without much thought. Notice the way you're holding your face now. Is it tense? Are your eyes squinted and focused on the words you're reading? How is your head tilted? Is your forehead tense and forward, or are you leaning back in bed?

Now, travel through the rest of your body.

What do you notice? It's easy to let tension build up in every crevice of our anatomy. Fidgeting with your hair or picking at your skin can be obvious signs of inner anxieties. A tense jaw and furrowed brow can go unnoticed by the person clenching these muscles, but the person they're having a conversation with might notice them before anything else.

Even if you aren't conscious of it, the person you're talking with can pick up on your anxieties through the way you might fidget or hold your shoulders. This could cause them to tense up in the same way, leading to a more strained conversation. Now both of you are anxious and unable to come up with anything to say, all because of unnecessary stress being passed between the two of you.

We have all had moments when we've walked into a room with choking tension. Whether you interrupted a serious conversation, or the people were gossiping about you, it's natural to pick up on signs from people even when they aren't speaking. To become an expert on these types of body language signals, you first need to understand and control your own. This starts small and builds overtime. Once you create a strong foundation for bodily reflection, you'll do it naturally, consistently maintaining control over your own body language.

One thing that can help control your body language is by practicing mindfulness techniques for relaxing your physical display. This starts with your breathing. Try a breathing exercise right now. Breathe in as you count to five, and then breathe out as you count down.

To catch your breath if you're breathing too fast, you can try an exercise by holding your breath for a moment, and then release it slowly:

1. Breathe in. Now count to one, two, three.

2. Let it out as you count four, five, six, seven, eight, nine, and ten.

This can reset your breathing when you're short of breath and panicking. If you ever feel light-headed while doing a breathing exercise, go a bit slower. There will be a release when you focus your breathing, but it shouldn't be to the point that it causes you to worry even more. As you manage your breathing, you can use these techniques while also controlling your body.

One of the best methods to familiarize yourself with your body is through a mindfulness scan. The steps are as follows

1. Lay down somewhere comfortable.

2. Release any strain or tension from your arms and limbs. Don't fold or bend your knees and elbows.

3. Start by noticing your head. Release any tension in it and let all your stress float out. Visualize it becoming more and more relaxed as you breathe in and out.

4. Repeat these exercises for each part of your body: face, neck, shoulders, chest, abdomen, hips, arms, elbows, hands, fingers, waist, thighs, knees, calves, shins, ankles, feet, and toes.

5. Go back up through your body the opposite way. Repeat this daily until you feel total relaxation.

This is a good practice to do every day, but below are some shorter mindfulness methods that you can do in just a few minutes, no matter where you are. Techniques like this relax your body by grounding you in the moment rather than running frantically through panicked thoughts that cause anxiety. These can be done before you arrive at the social event, during a break in the bathroom, or even while you're getting freshened up in the back of a taxi:

- Identify colors in the room

- Pick a calming color that makes you feel safe. Identify everything in the room that is this color. Repeat with different colors and materials like cloths, woods, and colorful plastics.

- Fingers and toes
    - Count and gently wiggle, tap, or move each finger and each toe where it's currently at. Repeat 5 times as you count through 100.

- Mindfulness object
    - Keep an object in your pocket at all times that you can refer to as your mindfulness object. Touch it when you are feeling nervous and use it as a reminder to stay grounded and focused on where you are and what you're doing. It could be a special coin or a small stone that you can squeeze for comfort when needed.

Read Their Mannerisms

Understanding the meaning behind smaller cues can help you better navigate conversations. When you're having moments of uncertainty, pay attention to how people are interacting with you and remind yourself that you're doing just fine. For example, if you think to yourself, "They're not interested in what I'm saying at all," you might notice they lean in. Then, they ask more questions, which is a sign that they clearly are interested in the things you're saying.

Alternatively, you can notice if this might actually be a sign that the conversation needs more work. For example, if they're leaning in repeatedly, it shows they want to hear what you're saying, but maybe they physically can't understand you because of a loud noise nearby. You can take this as a sign that they would agree to the suggestion of moving somewhere quieter. If they aren't interested and are looking around at the loud and bustling room, it could be a sign that now isn't the best time for an intimate conversation.

When you practice your own mindfulness, it can rub off on the other person. Noticing someone might be anxious or uncomfortable can be your chance to have some of your own self-reflection. Do some of those mindfulness techniques from earlier, like noticing your body or regulating your breath. After you do this, they might start picking up on these things, such as regulated breathing. Now the two of you are more relaxed and you can focus on improving the conversation. If they are really struggling to open up, you can integrate mindfulness into the conversation. For example, you might say something like, "Wow, the carpet has a really interesting color," or "I like the design of the windows in this building." When pointing directly to things in your surroundings, it draws their attention back to the present rather than wherever they might be in their head.

You can familiarize yourself with common body language signals to pay better attention to the things someone might be telling you beyond their words:

- Notice their eye contact

    o If someone is looking at the bar as you talk, maybe they need a refill. If they're looking at everyone who passes, they might be wanting to talk to someone specific. You can ask these things to help them search and have their needs met, building a relationship.

- Check their hands and their stance

    o Hands and feet can tell a lot about a person. If someone is scratching their head or shaking their leg, maybe they're a little nervous and need a break or a topic change. You can ask a new question or suggest walking somewhere else for a change of scenery if they're likely overwhelmed by their surroundings. Someone's hands clasped together might show they're feeling closed off and reserved. A hand over the mouth could mean they're holding back their thoughts. Asking a question could open them up. Feet pointed towards the door could be a sign that they're ready to leave.

- Consider personal space

    o Are they getting closer to you? This is a good sign they want to open up and connect even more. They feel safe and comfortable around you, so now could be a sign to open up more to them. Don't go too fast with this, however, as it might simply be a matter of space. Is someone moving away from you? Do they have their arms crossed and their torso turned in a direction away from you? It could be a sign that they aren't interested in the conversation and it's best to talk later.

- Hear the tone and volume of their voice

    o Talking loud and firm is a sign that they're engaged in the conversation. If they're speaking quietly and slowly, they could be lacking confidence. Mimic how they're talking in an intimate setting.

- Evaluate the style of their smile

    o Smiles are one of the strongest forms of unspoken language. Some smiles are fake and forced. These are smiles that might be a display of teeth or smiles in which the eyes stay the same. A more open mouth and crinkles around the eyes and cheeks indicate a more natural smile. It's important to know the difference between someone just being friendly and a person actually being interested in the conversation.

- Determine their participation level
    - Are you speaking over them too much? An encouraging statement or thought-provoking question could help open them up and lead to more participation on their end. If you're in a group setting, it's helpful to notice if one person is talking over someone else so you can back up that person who's struggling to share their thoughts. It leads to more trust and control over the discussion, helping you to lead it in the direction towards your success.

Mimic Their Body Language

Once you know how to read their body language, you'll be able to mimic it to have more control over the situation. When you think of mimicking, your first thought might go towards the idea of mocking someone in an insulting way. That's not the case; mimicking is just mirroring what the other person is displaying to help establish a connection. It builds a back and forth that helps open up the conversation to lead to greater outcomes.

For example, if they are sitting with their arms crossed, you can do the same. Then when you open your arms and relax, it will cause them to mimic you subconsciously, leading to a more relaxed environment. You're physically opening them up without even saying anything if you take this route during a conversation. It's not about controlling the situation in a negative way where you're manipulating someone else. It helps to create a standard of comfortability so you and the other person can share as much as possible, creating more meaningful discussions.

Mimicked body movement is a good sign that the other person is engaged in what you're saying. They might end up doing the same thing that you're conveying when they're really trusting of you. This is seen when someone else takes a drink of their water after you did, or maybe they lean against the wall in the same manner you are. Seeing small signs like this from the other person helps to build confidence while you're talking. You can then use this tactic to mimic the things they share, continuing that healthy repertoire.

Mirroring body language has been proven to have more positive returns for those who are intentionally mimicking the other person (Goman, 2011). A waitress that is open and laughing with customers might be more likely to get good tips than one who is closed off and hurried through body language. Establishing a personal connection in a situation like this makes the other person feel like they have a deeper connection. Playing into that person's empathy will lead to them providing more back, and in a situation like the one with the waitress, that results in a higher tip.

Fronting is a great way to square up with the other person. This puts your torso directly in front of theirs, creating a small space between the two of you. This blocks them from all other stimulation, allowing greater focus on each other rather than your surroundings. They will have a face-to-face connection with you, meaning you can take advantage of their full attention to have a moment to share your thoughts uninterrupted. It is like creating a blank slate to better mimic their body language.

Match their voice, volume, and tone. If someone is being quieter with you, they might be shy or perhaps they are trying to pull you in closer. They could be lacking confidence or trying to hide what they're saying from others in the room. Match their level to keep them comfortable. Matching their tone might not always be the best if you notice that they have a really stressed or angry tinge in their voice. In fact, doing the opposite is a good way to help them follow your cues. For example, if you notice they are getting really angry and working up over something, you might mimic their sentiment through a changed and more lighthearted tone, leading to the both of you laughing to break up some tension.

Nod often. It's like you're almost pulling information out of them by using your head and neck to make encouraging motions. You're breaking up some of the tension and adding a looseness and rhythm to the air, resulting in them matching your frequency. The thoughts will flow out of them, and they'll be more likely to share if you give nonverbal cues that you're listening to them.

Use your body for bigger reactions. If they tell you something shocking and all you can say is, "wow," you could take a step back or open your arms. Not only does this give you a moment to think of how to respond, but it could lead to them sharing even more information during your display of reaction.

Change your body language when they change tones. Maybe you made a joke that didn't land in a more serious situation. Quickly recover by matching that acknowledged tone rather than doubling down and making more jokes. This could only cause further awkwardness in the conversation and setting. If they become more lighthearted, maybe it's your cue to loosen up a bit.

Hand them something if you really want to open them up. For example, handing a beverage to them as soon as a conversation starts can be a way to establish trust immediately. Rather than sitting there with their arms crossed awkwardly, they now have something to focus on while also feeling comforted by your hospitality.

The steps to having good body language when small talking include

1. Paying attention to your own body language.

2. Noticing the body language of the other person(s).

3. Mimicking body language to create a positive outcome.

Beyond the bodies, you have to consider what fills the space not only between, but also around your bodies to get the best outcome possible from your small-talk-filled conversations.

Prepare the Setting

Think of your favorite place. Maybe it's your couch snuggled up next to your loved ones, your favorite lamp glowing through the room and a hand knit blanket draped around your shoulders. Perhaps it's your garden, butterflies dancing through flowers as wind blows leaves to create a harmonic scene.

The location you're in can drastically change how you feel. The ice white dentist's office or a brightly lit government office can make us feel the opposite of how we feel in our favorite place.

Try to research the area you're going to before you arrive. If it's a place you're already familiar with, like your boss's office, it might enable you to feel more comfortable in this space and have an idea for what to do when the day comes to have an important conversation.

If you're arriving at an event before someone else, consider how you want to be positioned so you can have a good conversation. For example, maybe you choose to face the entrance so that your conversing companion's back is to the crowd, and the only thing to look at is you and the wall. This way, they will focus more on what you have to say rather than being distracted by those entering and exiting. If you want to have a more intimate conversation with someone, you might choose a booth or table out of the way of chaos.

You can also keep this in consideration for when you're arriving somewhere alone and want to meet up with people to socialize with quickly. Don't wait by the door; people will pass by quickly. This is a good spot to hangout if you're hosting and want to give everyone a brief greeting. If you want to link up with people and have a good conversation, hanging out near the bar is a good option. If you don't really know anybody, look for big groups. There's a chance that many people are quiet and listening to one other person, allowing you to join in easier. If you approach a group of two people, they might be in an intimate conversation.

If you're hosting, there are many things you can do to prepare the setting so that you and the other person have an amazing conversation. Choosing to host gives you a little more control in the situation, which is why it can be a good choice for those who are feeling extra nervous. You can offer to meet at a restaurant you're familiar with, where you're more likely to feel comfortable at your favorite table. Hosting at home will allow you to be even more in tune with your surroundings, but there are still a few important things to remember to get the mood just right:

- Bright lights might make someone tense up. Pick the right lighting to set the mood. Lamps are more intimate than overhead lights. Candles can add warmth and a cozy touch to colder spaces (just make sure to practice fire safety, especially in larger groups). Colorful lights can enhance the mood even further. For example, purple can add a friendly feeling. Changing lights will give the place more of a *party* feel, great for loosening things up.

- Match the setting to the mood you want them to feel when talking. If it's an important meeting when everyone should be alert and serious, an office setting with a bright overhead light is best. If it's a casual meeting between friends catching up, a cozy bar after dinner might set the tone better.

- Get information on what everyone's food and drink preferences are. Whether someone has special dietary requirements or allergies, it's good hosting etiquette to ensure everyone's needs are met. Paying attention to their favorites can also help. For example, if your boss loves cherries and you make a cherry pie for dessert, it's a personal way to show you listen well when having conversations.

- Curate a playlist if you'll have control over the music. If it's a large event with many types of people, an evergreen jazz might do best. A more exciting party could have crowd-pleasing classics. Dinner at your apartment might do best with a casual playlist curated to show your tastes. Get creative and make sure to adjust accordingly.

- Ensure there is enough seating for everyone. This is especially true for an event when there will be a meal, viewing, or speech of some sort. Standing in the back is sometimes expected, but for longer events, make sure everyone has a spot they can sit comfortably.

- Is there an activity or a focus that everyone will participate in? It might be a good idea to have a game prepared, or something to watch and reference depending on the goals of the conversation. If the conversation starts to dry out and more awkward air is present, a planned activity can break things up.

- Consider weather factors. Will they need a place to wipe their feet? Will there be a safe place for coats and purses? This can help avoid initial awkward moments upon arrival.

Cleaning up is usually a sign that the party is over. If you have some guests overstaying their welcome, you can politely prompt them. You might ask if they'd like any leftovers. You could take their empty drinks and do some light cleaning/organizing so they get the hint.

Always be respectful of the space around you. Your guests represent you when you are the host, so ensure to keep things clean and organized after the event.

Chapter 4:

Conversation Topics

At the core of every great conversation is an interesting topic. Not only that, but it must also be something open-ended to keep the conversation going. Once you've worked through your anxieties and started to build important confidence, the progress doesn't stop there. Having ideas of great conversation topics will help to create a natural flow so the conversation is long-lasting and helps you to get closer to your goals.

The next four techniques include

1. Asking a lot of questions to keep the conversation flowing.

2. Repeating what the speaker says shows you're listening and helps to keep things moving.

3. Open-ended answers also give you the chance to keep the conversation going.

4. Great discussions can be created by identifying where you and the speaker connect and differ.

Ask a Lot of Questions

The best kind of questions are those that are open-ended. An open-ended conversation is one that invites discussion. It goes beyond just asking a question that can be responded to with a singular phrase. Asking simple yes or no questions will lead to a dead conversation. Too many yes or no questions can make the conversation feel interrogative and high pressure. It's simple to change a yes or no question into an open-ended one with a few word twists. Look at the examples below:

Yes/No Question	Open-Ended Question
Did you have a good day?	What did you get into today?
Do you have any plans for the weekend?	What are your plans for this weekend?
Are you enjoying your dinner?	What's your favorite dish tonight?
Did you find the place ok?	How did you get here, and did it go smoothly?

Asking also helps encourage the other person to take on more of the conversation. If you ask how they got there and they have a story about how they missed two trains, that will lead to them opening up and sharing more. If they don't answer with much, that still gives you more to go off, or you can answer yourself. For example, if you ask what their plans are for the weekend and they say, "nothing much," you can respond with your plans while addressing their answer. You might say, "Sounds like a great weekend, mine is going to be really busy!"

This could also lead into a suggestion to open up another conversation. You might say, "Oh, if you're looking for something to do, I saw this amazing movie last weekend," or "I tried this great, new taco place you should check out if you need a bite to eat." The conversation has then been opened up to a new topic, like the other restaurants they like or movies they've seen.

Open-ended questions also help to fill air when you don't know what to transition to next. In between bites and drinks, you might ask some questions to your dinner date:

- Have you traveled recently or are you looking to soon?
- What's a good restaurant you've been to recently?

- What was the last great meal you had?

When coming up with questions on the spot, use the five Ws: who, what, where, when, and why. For example, if they say, "My husband is in Chicago this week," the *who* is the husband, but you can also ask, "Who did they go with?" or "Who are they visiting?"

Next ask the other Ws. What is the occasion? Why did they go? Where are they staying? When are they coming home? Of course, you don't want to quiz them in a repetitive pattern. Not only can it cause them even more anxiety, but it could show that you're not really listening or intrigued and instead just going through the motions.

Sometimes, you'll just have to memorize questions to use as you're getting to know people. Keep it fun and creative. Following these prompts will give you plenty of new conversational paths to follow:

- What are your pet peeves?
- What are your guilty pleasures?
- What would you change about your community?
- What would you do if you won the lottery?
- What's your most embarrassing memory?
- What's a childhood memory that makes you nostalgic?
- Do you remember the first movie or show you watched?
- What three items would you take to a deserted island?
- Would you repeat high school if you could?
- What would you do as president?
- What would you do if the world was ending?
- Who would you call if you were in trouble?

- What's an animal that best describes you?
- What's your biggest dream?
- What's your biggest fear?

You'll want to be careful to not make it feel like you're grilling the other person. It will cause them to freeze up and think too hard about their answers. If you notice that they aren't giving you much to go off and are withholding, back off a little. They might be feeling self-conscious and would prefer to not talk. You can then work through this by sharing your own information. Answer the questions that they didn't want to fully answer.

When you distract them in this way, they will feel more comfortable sharing. You can dig deeper in the conversation because it shows a shared connection between two parties rather than a cold delivered interview. They'll open up and will start to ask more questions, giving you even more ideas to keep tossing back the other way.

Rephrase What They Said

Whether you're completely blanking on what to say next, or you just started a conversation, one of the best tips to follow is to rephrase what they said. This means taking the exact statement they said and sometimes repeating it back to them word for word. For example, if they say, "I'm going to Paris tomorrow," you might say back to them, "You're going to Paris tomorrow?" with an enthusiastic tone.

If you use that and an excited tone, it helps build them up. They'll feel more confident, and it shows that you want to hear what they have to share. From there, they'll continue to go into more details about their trip. This puts all of the conversation pressure on them, because now they're the ones who have to talk about themselves.

Your tone can really change the outcome and that will be the main way that you rephrase the things they're saying in a conversation. If somebody says something that can call you to action, like, "I haven't eaten all day," you might say back to them, "Oh my gosh, you haven't eaten all day?" a little bit slower and more dramatic. It helps highlight their point, show that you really care about their feelings, and that you connect with the things that they're sharing. You can then redirect the focus towards getting them something to eat. Maybe you can take your conversation to a restaurant, and now you have a more intimate setting where you can talk one on one with the other person. You might also help them find where to get food at the actual event. You can walk them to a vending machine or food stand within a convention, meaning you will have longer to talk to them rather than just sending them on their way.

Even if they only say a quick, "yeah," in response to your repetition, you can still have more time to think of what to say. For example, if somebody shares something personal with you like, "I just found out my sister is going to have a baby." You can say, "Wow, that's amazing. Your sister is going to have a baby! You're going to be an aunt or an uncle!" They might just simply say, "Yeah, it's really exciting," and not really go into more details. However, this still gives you a moment to pause and think about what else you can bring up next. You might say, "Wow, is this her first baby?" or "Is she excited?"

You can ask about their thoughts and opinions. If they don't really give you much to go on, it might be a sign that they don't want to talk about this right now, so you can move on. You can still use that to relate to your own experiences. For example, if you ask if she's excited, what she's naming the baby, or if she's having a boy or a girl, you might not get any responses. They might blow through the conversation and not really want to discuss anything baby related. You can relate this to your own experience. Maybe you share something like, "My cousin just had a little baby girl named Angela. She is so cute. It is such a joy to have kids in the picture." Find a way you can relate to this with your own experiences after they have signaled that they might not want to talk about it too much. Chances are they will open up and share more about this experience with you.

Sharing these things can help open the doors to new conversations and connections. Rephrasing what they said also helps you better remember the things that you're talking about. If somebody shares with you, "I have 15 projects coming up that I really want you to work on," you can say, "Wow, 15 projects? That sounds like a great plan!"

Not only does it help you remember that information, but you also reassure the other person that you're listening and that you know what's going on. It signals that they can continue to share things with you because you are going to reciprocate within the conversation.

Give Open-Ended Answers

Just like you have to ask open-ended questions, it's also important to give open-ended answers. Sometimes, it can be hard to do this because we can feel put on the spot. You might suddenly be overcome with the pressure to say something interesting to keep the conversation moving. While it can be stress-inducing for some people, it's also essential that you make sure you don't cut the conversation short and let dead air rise.

This was one of my biggest mistakes when participating in small talk. I felt the pressure from somebody else's question, and it made me feel like I needed to come up with an amazing conversation topic and give them a colorful, exciting answer.

In reality, you are both tossing a ball back and forth. They're not throwing the ball hard. This isn't a game of dodgeball—you don't have to dodge their questions. It's when one person shares a small tidbit, and then the other person does, and over time, that sharing speeds up and becomes more fluid.

If I had a really bad week during which I didn't leave the house much and I didn't get much done, I might have been feeling bad about myself. Then when somebody asked how my week was, I would clam up and say nothing. I would say, "I didn't really do anything," and all of a sudden it would make me think about how I felt like I was not good enough. I started to feel all my insecurities about how I needed to leave the house more, make more friends, and to get out there and try new things. All of a sudden, I was spiraling and all they were trying to do was start a conversation.

They weren't quizzing me. They weren't going to grill me about how much work I got done. They weren't going to mock me or make fun of me for not going out at all. They weren't going to poke fun and make me feel bad for not eating out at a restaurant, meeting up with friends, or doing anything else interesting. They simply were trying to start a conversation.

What I could have said instead in these scenarios is "Oh, not much. Honestly, it was a really slow week. I just focused on resting. How about you?"

Sometimes they might want to share what they were going through that weekend. They might not know what else to talk about or do not want to bring it up themselves. You can toss the ball gently back to them and keep up a nice, consistent, and even repertoire.

This can feel awkward at first, but with time, you'll get better. Before you know it, you will be the one asking questions and keeping the flow going. It's not a bad thing to not have an answer, and one-word responses are still needed at times. Just keep in mind that your answers should at least help facilitate some form of back and forth.

If they ask, "How are you doing today?" The quick response is to say, "I'm fine." Consider these topics to explore as you develop your response:

- Trace all the way back to when you woke up.
    - Did you wake up on time? Did you wake up feeling good? Did you have an easy morning? What did you have for breakfast?
- Take it to lunch.
    - Did you meet somebody for lunch? Did you try a new recipe? Did you hear anything interesting on the news? Did you take your dog for a walk? Did you talk to a

friend? Did you listen to any good music? Did you pass by an interesting, new store on the street?

Whatever small thing you did in your day can be used to spark a conversation. It helps to be mindful as you're going throughout your day to think about these things that you could bring up in a discussion later. They might never become conversation topics, but that doesn't mean you can't still acknowledge them so that you're prepared. For example, if you try a new place for lunch, you can take note of that and mention it to somebody later. Think of the things that you enjoy: Did you see a good movie or hear a good song? These can be things that you recommend to other people. You might tell somebody, "Oh, I've been listening to this song on repeat, and it's been stuck in my head all day."

Our daily tasks can be good starters for conversations and at the very least, lead into a discussion. They're not asking for you to give them a handwritten schedule of every single task you did that day. They just want to spark a conversation.

When you genuinely can't think of anything else to say, you can still make a comment about that. Phrase it in a longer way, such as, "It feels like I did a lot, but I really can't think of anything crazy that happened. I'm feeling kind of brain dead lately. I'm really tired."

You don't have to go into detail about how you've been struggling or procrastinating. Everyone has ups and downs, so don't make yourself feel bad. There are more things to talk about in your life than you realize. It's just easy to forget these little details as we repeat habits throughout our day.

Sometimes people aren't trying to start a conversation and they are genuinely being friendly. If the checkout cashier at the store asks, "How are you today?" They're not asking for your backstory. They are being polite. These are small gestures. Still, it's important to know the difference between when somebody genuinely wants to start a conversation and when they are saying things to help pass the time.

Identify Interests and Dislikes

Before and during the conversation, find differences and similarities that you and the other person have. This can create an entirely new world of conversation topics. Sometimes small talk can feel unnecessary. Does the awkward silence in an elevator really need to be filled? That depends on the situation. Every person can offer insight into who they are by sharing interesting information that you might not have ever discovered had you not given the effort to chat with them up.

Of course, stray away from anything too serious, like politics or religion. We'll discuss more topics that you shouldn't discuss during small talk in a later section.

Identifying small differences can become a way to relate to one another. For example, you might be standing outside when the snow starts to fall. Perhaps they say, "Oh, I hate the snow." Maybe you respond, "Oh, I actually don't mind it, but I can definitely see how it's frustrating for people to deal with."

Now you've both shared an experience with each other, even though there are differences. You can start a conversation about why they dislike snow and why you like it. It's not anything to take personal offense from. Some people actually connect through their differences. And as a general rule, weather is a safe small talk topic.

You can also make small observations about your surrounding environment. It's important to always stay positive and never be too negative. However, sometimes you might find that you may connect with someone else based on the things you complain about. For example, if somebody is rubbing their shoulders or shivering, you might say, "Yeah, it is a little too cold in here, isn't it? I wonder if there's somebody we can talk to about adjusting the temperature?"

You're establishing a connection with them beyond this similarity. If somebody is picking around their plate and pushing their olives to the side, you can make a small joke like, "I don't really like olives either."

It's not about hating these things or gossiping about people. It's making small observations about things that you can connect with, because sometimes we feel more comfortable opening up and complaining about things than being positive. Saying, "Oh, that movie was great," is easy, but sometimes it can be hard to pick out the things that you actually liked about it. If you watch a movie with somebody that was absolutely awful, you could probably talk all night about all the weird things in the film, from the awkward acting to the terrible ending.

Go through and identify the things that you both like.

If they're wearing a purple sparkly dress, you can say, "I love purple and glitter!" Then you can start talking about your wardrobes. If they give you a compliment, then you can also take the opportunity to see if they share that similarity. If they say, "I love your shoes," you can say, "Oh, thank you. I absolutely love this brand. Have you tried it before?" This conversation could lead down many paths.

You can also simply make declarations of things that you love. If you are standing in a bar and looking out the front window, you might see a little dog pass by. You can say something like, "Oh, I just love small dogs." They might say the same. Maybe they say, "Oh, my sister has an adorable little dog." Then they pull up pictures on their phone, and before you know it, you two are talking about dogs for the next hour. A whole conversation can stem from a quick observation about a dog that passes by.

You can say this with dislikes, too. Maybe you're staring out the window and it starts raining. You might say, "Oh man, I really hate the rain." They might also share that same opinion and again, you are both connecting on things that you dislike. It's also interesting and can keep things exciting when you identify things that one of you likes and the other one hates. Again, keep it civil and avoid conflict if you do notice that there's some tension being created between you and the other person.

In a situation like this, it's essential that you never make the other person feel bad about what they like. It's a phrase referred to as, "Don't yuck my yum." If a commercial comes on for a TV show that you absolutely hate, they might declare that they love that show and that they haven't been able to stop watching it. It can be easy to react with your true opinion right away, but all this is going to do is make them feel bad. Why would you want to make somebody else feel bad about the things that they like? You don't have to lie and pretend like you actually like the show. You can simply approach the topic with a little curiosity and understanding. You might say something like, "Oh, I actually didn't really get into that. I watched a few episodes, but it wasn't really my style." Maybe they then say, "Oh, I totally agree. I definitely could see how somebody might not be into it. I just have a connection to it because it reminds me of my hometown or my childhood."

They may also share insight with you as to why they like it. They might say something like, "Oh yeah, it is kind of hard for people to watch. But I think the director was really making it in a funny way that's meant to be more of a parody than something serious." They could present a new way of better understanding this program that they're sharing. You could also talk about shows that you enjoy to see if there's a program you can both relate to.

Chapter 5:

Before the Conversation

Being prepared for a specific conversation should never be overlooked. While some will pop up unexpectedly, having a head start into the conversation makes you feel more comfortable so you can navigate through it successfully. The final preparation techniques are

1. Research the location, people, and other relevant information before the chat.

2. Be conscious of topics to avoid so you can prevent awkwardness and conflict.

3. Practice warm-up techniques so your voice is ready to go.

4. Be prepared in the event that the conversation goes wrong, so you can rein it back in.

Do Your Research

A big part of being prepared for a social interaction is knowing where you're going. Whether it's a cool bar you're meeting new friends at or the largest convention center in America, knowing a little about the background of these locations can assist you when it comes time to think of small talk topics.

Research where you will be. It might be a cool historic building and that could be a conversation topic. Maybe there's an urban legend about the place or a famous celebrity who has been there before. Having small fun facts about the place or the location can give you topics to discuss with people you've never even met before. Go beyond the location. Maybe there's a cool train that passes by the area or a historic landmark down the street. Even though you're not directly in the building, you can still reference it by saying something like, "I passed the hotel that Marilyn Monroe used to stay at all the time on my way here." Something short and easy like this can lead to many different types of conversations.

Stay up to date on current events so you can keep up with certain conversations. This would be things like state, country, and global news. It's good to familiarize yourself with general news topics of places you're going to as well. For example, if you're headed to Boston from your hometown of Los Angeles, you might discover that Boston has a big election coming up. Though you don't plan to vote for anyone since you don't live there, having an idea of who the politicians involved are can help you keep up with conversations if it gets brought up by locals.

Familiarize yourself with these topics, but don't try too hard to memorize facts. You don't need to study the history of Boston politics. A quick Google search and article skim while you're waiting to board your plane can give you a leg up when interacting with local Bostonians. Not only will you have a better grasp on the conversation they're having, making you look more interested, but you will also be able to use these things as ways to lead into other conversations that you can be a bigger part of.

It's okay to not form an opinion. In fact, researching both sides can help you have a better grasp on what the other person might end up sharing. Forming too strong of an opinion can blind you. You'll end up forming an emotional tie to the conversation, making it harder to navigate it in an objective way. You don't want to get into an argument with someone you just met about an opinion you just formed.

If you do form a strong opinion, understand how to share these thoughts without hurting the other person. If you find out that one of the Boston politicians is the evilest candidate you've ever heard of and the four new people you just met all love him, it might be hard to *not* get emotional. However, this is why skimming information can suit you better. You can segue the conversation away from this emotional topic by saying something like, "I heard he went to Boston University, where did you all go?"

Use these research skills to get to know the people you're interacting with better as well. You might ask where they live, or the kind of transportation they used to get there. Ask simple questions like, "Are you from around here?" or "Did you fly or drive in?" This can lead to a conversation about their hometown, or maybe they have a funny story about their plane ride over.

Ask about their friends and family. Are they a father of five? Do they live with roommates? Do they have a bunch of college friends they hang out with? You can phrase this in a casual way, such as, "Do you have family here?" or "I bet your family misses you while you're so far away." They can then share stories about how they're visiting their mom, or how they left their kids at home with a babysitter. Things could get a little awkward if they don't have friends or family, but you can transition into other topics quickly by asking about pets or if they travel frequently.

Give the menu a glance before you go. This research is important so that you can focus on the conversation and what's actually happening around you rather than trying to figure out what to order. You can also read restaurant reviews to see what's good. This can be a topic to discuss. For example, you might say something like, "It seems like they're known for their steak," or "If we have room after dinner, we should try a slice of their world-famous cheesecake."

Notice the weather and what the upcoming trends are going to be. This can prepare you to dress accordingly. Though it might feel warm when you leave your hotel room, you don't want to be trapped outside in a late-night snowstorm.

Other topics might include

- Travel
    - What are recent trends in traveling? Is everyone going to the Bahamas? Is everyone flocking to Hawaii? You can also ask others where they plan to travel.

- Local sports
    - Knowing the major teams and how they're doing can be enough to keep you an active part of a conversation.
- Local art and music
    - Familiarizing yourself with these topics gives you the chance to ask more questions about people's preferences while also sharing suggestions of your own.
- Related celebrities
    - A clothing convention might be filled with people up to date on who wore the best outfits at the city's recent fashion week. A journalism conference could bring about topics of local writers and news anchors, and the things they are reporting on.

Know What Topics to Avoid

Politics, religion, past trauma, and other emotionally charged subjects might be too much depending on the conversation. There are also ways to approach these topics if you are in a context when those things might get brought up.

Bringing up politics and religion can either polarize a conversating group or pull them together. However, since they are based so heavily on the belief system we use to operate, there's no way of knowing which way someone might swing—either towards or away from your own personal perspective.

At the same time, since so much of our point of view is dependent on these things, the topics can get very emotional. It's best to avoid them, and if you notice they're getting brought up frequently, it might require a total subject change to ensure conflict doesn't arise.

If these two hot topics are the focus of your small talk situations, then learning to navigate these in a civil way is important. For example, a political convention or a religious meet up are bound to touch on these topics. Remember to not get too worked up if someone disagrees when discussing these things. You probably won't change someone's stance, especially if it turns into an argument. If you want to share an opposing viewpoint, you might start your phrase with something like

- have you considered

- from my experience I've realized

- I had similar viewpoints as you until I thought about

Remember to not take it personally at the end of the day. Other people have entirely different lives, and their political and religious viewpoints may go much deeper than your own.

Avoid bringing up gossip about the people that you're around. Not only is it risky, as someone might end up overhearing you, but it could make you look bad. You might end up saying something that's received a little harsher than it sounded in your head, or maybe you accidentally make a comment about someone else that the person you're talking to knows. If other people bring up the gossip first, it can be hard to not partake, especially if you have something to share. However, you still put yourself at risk, so it's best to not discuss anything and instead smile, nod, and try to redirect the conversation.

Keep conversations PG-movie-rating compliant, meaning no mention of sex or drugs. Alcohol might be brought up, but it should be *part* of the conversation, not the *center* of it. Even though everyone is holding a glass of wine, it might not be the best time to discuss how hungover you were the other day.

Death and illness might be topics that can bring down the mood. Of course, they are a real part of life, so when they get brought up, approach them with sensitivity. You don't need to go into details. For example, if you ask how your coworker's husband is doing, she might tell you, "Really bad actually, he was just diagnosed with stage 4 cancer." At that point, you will want to overload her with sympathy.

Say something about how sorry you are to hear that and that you're always going to be there to offer support, but only if you truly feel that way. Don't offer future help if you're not able to provide it. This will help validate her feelings and let her know that you genuinely care about how he is doing. Unless she brings it up first, you don't want to ask for details about his treatments or symptoms. It could make her uncomfortable and upset.

It's important for you to also avoid trauma dumping. Trauma dumping is when you share your difficult experiences with someone else in a situation when they might not be expecting it or aren't prepared to handle it. It can be easy to do this after a few too many drinks, and sometimes it's automatic when we're already feeling vulnerable and nervous. Not only can trauma dumping make the other person uncomfortable, but they might not have the reaction that we need to feel validated about sensitive situations we've been through. When having a really deep, connecting conversation with someone else, it can be hard to put a limit on how much you're sharing. When you meet someone that you can open up with, there's an excitement that can make us want to lay it all out for them to see. However, if you're not careful, this can lead to trauma dumping.

If you find yourself trauma dumping often, it might mean you need more emotional support from the people in your life, whether it be professional or through those who are closest to you. After you find you've compulsively trauma dumped, remember that someone else's reaction doesn't have to define how you should feel about that situation. You can move on quickly and change the subject as you would in any other uncomfortable scenario.

This doesn't mean you can't ever share some of your traumas. It's just about ensuring that you do so in a safe environment where the other person has consented to it, is ready to hear about this trauma in a safe way, and when they feel they can offer support and feedback.

Some specific situations call for specific topics to avoid. For example, if you're talking with a new coworker, you might connect on the fact that you both are going through divorces. However, a first date isn't the time to air your frustrations with the person you just broke up with last week.

Money can be a sensitive topic around coworkers. It can come off poorly to others, especially if they're having a rough time with money. Don't brag about going on vacation to the employees whose hours you just had to cut. Sure, maybe someone else is paying for the trip, but it can be a sensitive topic to discuss.

Warm-Up Before the Conversation

Think of your favorite musician right now. Whether it's a pop star or the lead singer of a band, they have to warm up before their performances. If you were to watch a documentary on one of their concerts, there would surely be a scene where they're backstage, doing warm-up exercises. Often these are harmony exercises that put them in the right tune or pitch for their performance.

While it might seem like something that only needs to be done for musical talent, you should be warming up before your conversations as well. This is especially true if you live alone and don't talk to anyone all day up until a big convention or party. What you might realize when you get there is that your voice is quiet and strained, leaving you feeling overwhelmed. This can create even more tension and anxiety. If you give yourself the opportunity to warm-up before you get there, you will realize that it's a lot easier to use your voice and hear your own words being said out loud.

Practice using your voice before the conversation in whatever way you can. This is true for somebody going on a first date or somebody giving a huge presentation to a large room filled with people. No matter the seriousness of the conversation, warming up your voice is still important because your vocal cords are a muscle. This muscular system within your throat needs to be stretched like any other muscle.

If you were to go run down the street, you would want to stretch your calves and your legs. If you were to lift heavy objects, you might stretch your arms and your chest. Warming up these muscles not only makes the process more comfortable, but it prevents potential injury. If you are going to be giving a big speech, it's crucial that you warm-up your voice so that your voice is not cracking and breaking the entire time that you're giving this presentation.

Warming up also includes warming up your body. This means stretching your legs, arms, and letting the blood flow through your body. When you stretch and feel your muscles, you become more relaxed. It takes some of that stiffness out of your body. It gives you the opportunity to feel more at peace and more connected with your physical anatomy. This will help your body language in ways that you won't realize until after your presentation or conversation is over.

Start by stretching your face and body muscles. This means squeezing your cheeks, lifting your eyebrows, and opening your mouth as wide as you can. Open your eyes as wide as you can like you just heard shocking news. Twist your face to reflect a few other emotions, like confusion, frustration, and realization.

Gently stretch your neck by slowly rolling your head around on your shoulders in a circle. Place your fists on your lower back and lean backwards. This will really open up your chest, a vulnerable position that can make you feel more comfortable later on.

Turn your head from side to side and try to twist your torso as well. Stretch your arms. Bend your elbows out in front of you and try to touch them together. This is a great way to stretch your shoulders and chest, which are necessary for open discussions.

Shake your limbs to feel some of that energy be released. Bend over, touch your toes, and stretch your legs and calf muscles. Feel the tension release from every part of your body.

Again, pay attention to how you're holding tension in your body right now. Even though we've already mentioned doing this in a previous section, you might have immediately gone back to holding tension in your face or shoulders once again.

Are you squinting? Are you following your brow? Are you sucking on your cheeks? Are you biting your tongue? What kind of tense things are you holding in your body right now?

You're not even talking to somebody else. You're simply doing some research and studying and you're still holding on to the stress and anxiety. Imagine how much you are exuding to the other person when you're in a conversation. Somebody with social anxiety is already going to be a little bit more on edge than somebody who might not have these types of struggles, meaning your tension is going to be worsened when you are discussing things with other people.

Stretch out your body and release all of this anxiety that's building up inside of you. Next, try saying short phrases that will get your voice warmed up. Try saying things like "ma-ma" and "wa-wa." It can feel silly, especially if you're alone or standing in front of your mirror doing it. However, it will make all the difference later on when you're having conversations. You're warming your voice up so that things come out smoother and so it feels more natural to you.

After that, blow air out through a small hole in your mouth. You can also make humming noises like "hmm" and "mmm." These are very simple things that can make you feel more comfortable with using your vocal cords. Picture air traveling from your mouth through your chest and back through your abdomen.

As you're breathing in and out and visualizing the air passing through your body, you'll feel more connected with your physical anatomy. Notice your posture and continue to stretch your muscles every time you feel them becoming tense again. Roll your shoulders backwards away from you as a way to help release them a little bit more.

If you go somewhere late at night and you haven't spoken all day, you might sit down and immediately feel stiff. You feel awkward and tense and you don't know what to do. Alternatively, you might feel a sudden burst of energy, causing you to talk too much and release a lot onto other people as you urgently open up from a long day inside.

Before the party, however, you can warm-up. Maybe you do this before or after your shower. You don't have to exercise for 30 minutes (though that also could help). All you have to do is stretch your body and breathe in while counting your breaths. Feel your muscles become more relaxed and let your body release all of that tension. Not only is this going to make you appear more relaxed, but it also gives you a chance to be mindful, so your brain stops ruminating about all the fears you have for the upcoming event.

Another great way that you can warm-up is by talking to people beforehand. If you are going to a big event later in the day, you might call a friend or a family member so that you can talk on the phone. This is enough to hear your voice out loud and get used to talking. Stop and get some coffee before the event and ask the barista how their day is going. You can chat them up to practice so that when it comes time to actually have important discussions, you feel more comfortable using your voice.

Talk to yourself in the mirror to get used to the way that you're using your hands and body while you talk. Smile at yourself, too. This can also act as a warm-up to relieve tension by seeing your own smile in the mirror. Make sure that your breath smells good. It's important to invest in a tongue scraper and mouthwash. Having gum and mints on you at all times is also an important way to make sure that you're not scaring people away with your stinky breath.

Stay hydrated throughout the day and carry water with you. When you are practicing all day and using your voice a lot, it can really dry you out. Speaking uses some of the moisture in our body as it's released through the hot air that we breathe talking. You'll notice yourself becoming dehydrated a lot faster on the days that you do a lot of talking versus the days where you're alone and not saying things as frequently. Keeping water on you can make sure that you never get tongue tied from being a little bit dry mouthed.

Say "hello" and "hi" to people right away. Smiling is nice but practicing an out loud "hello" can help with your confidence as you warm up to a new environment.

Be Prepared if It Goes Wrong

Not all conversations will go smoothly no matter how prepared we are. Know what to do when silence starts, when an uncomfortable subject gets brought up, or even if you say something you shouldn't have. Learning to recover will make these moments much easier to manage.

One of the most helpful techniques to master is knowing what to do when the conversation goes wrong. You can prepare yourself with statements that will lighten the mood and pull you out of awkward conversations.

One of my favorite phrases to have on hand is, "That is interesting."

This is useful in any situation, whether somebody is complaining and making the situation awkward, or they tell you something that you have no idea how to react to. "That's interesting," is a blanket statement. Everything in life is interesting if you really think about it. Even a menial task like brushing your teeth is interesting. Who decided that we needed to start brushing our teeth? Think of other amazing ways that there are to brush your teeth. Tying your shoes is interesting. Who came up with these methods? Who is the first person that ever tied their shoes? Any subject can become interesting to an interesting person, so this is a good phrase to go to that will help you and the other person begin reflecting.

It's a great way to keep the conversation lighthearted and flowing if things do get a little awkward. It's a way to approach a question that you don't know how to answer. If somebody asks you, "What is the hardest accomplishment you've ever achieved in a professional setting?" It might take a minute to think about it. Whether you have a million accomplishments and you can't narrow them down, or your mind is completely blank and you can't remember any of your accomplishments, you can respond by saying, "That's an interesting question, let me think." It's a phrase that buys you time.

It's also a great way to give a compliment when you're not sure what to say. If somebody shows you their new short film and you think it's the worst thing you've ever seen, you might not want to share that right away. Instead, you might say, "Wow, that was so interesting." You can then buy yourself some time to think about some of the smaller details of the film that you did like, such as saying, "I really liked the lighting" or "It was really detailed." It's not that you're lying, but sometimes there will be situations that throw us off and having evergreen statements ready can help you prepare.

When an awkward conversation happens, you can also focus on complimenting somebody. Maybe you're the host, and you made all the cookies for the event. As you're standing around with somebody they blurt out, "These cookies are terrible." It might make things really awkward. They might not realize that you're the one who made the cookies, and you might feel a little bit hurt. You might be feeling a little sensitive because they just said something really mean about something you put a lot of effort into. While it might be uncomfortable, lashing out and yelling at them can make things even worse. What you could do instead is compliment them and say something like, "I appreciate how bold you are," or "I like that you aren't afraid to share what's on your mind." It might sound a little passive aggressive if not said in the right tone, but still, it's better than being directly aggressive.

You can also redirect the conversation to somebody else when you might be struggling to come up with your own thoughts. For example, maybe somebody is sharing a long story. At the end you realize that you kind of zoned out and weren't fully paying attention and they turn to you and say, "What do you think about that?"

You might be frozen because you realize that you weren't listening to their story. You can then turn to somebody else and say something kind of generic like the blanket statement I mentioned earlier. For example, if they turn to you and say, "So, what do you think about that story there?" you might say, "Oh my, that is so interesting. I cannot believe that. You've left me speechless! Jim, what do you think?" Then you turn to somebody else and make the conversation go towards them. Remember that tossing the ball analogy? Sometimes we're thrown into situations like hot potato, so tossing it to someone else can be your method of choice when times call for it.

Sometimes conversations just get awkward because we don't know how to react, especially when somebody is sharing something that we have no knowledge about. For example, if you walk into a conversation with two coworkers and they're talking about the cars they're fixing up, you might feel completely isolated. You have no idea what is involved in the process of making a car and you can't contribute to this conversation at all. Even if you have nothing else to say you can ask other people for their knowledge and advice. You might say, "Oh, wow, how'd you get into that?"

You can make the environment a little more playful as well. You might play a guessing game. If you walk into a conversation and notice that somebody needs a drink, you could make a playful joke like, "Do you want me to grab you a fresh one? Wait, let me guess what you're drinking tonight... A negroni?" It can keep the air lighthearted when things are feeling a little tense.

Having an activity as a backup can also ensure that there's something to go to when you need to change topics. If people are coming over for a party, then it's a good idea to have some games on hand. You don't have to make this the focus of the night and you don't have to force anybody to play a game if they don't want to. However, having this ready is a way to have a go-to when there is an awkward moment or if the direction of the conversation needs to change. It can be a great way to break the ice. Think of easy to learn group games. You don't want to play something hard that has a ton of rules like Catan or Risk. These are better for more intimate situations when your sole focus is to play games for a few hours. Think of easy games like Jenga, or many different card games that people can casually play with time commitments of 20 minutes or less.

When all else fails, exit in an endearing or helpful way. You might say something like "Well, on that note, I'm going to run to the restroom."

If things get really awkward, you could say, "Well then! How about we get some refills?" It's a way to acknowledge that the conversation got a little awkward without just walking away, leaving the other person feeling even more uncomfortable.

Chapter 6:

During the Conversation

Now that you've worked through your main issues and prepared for the conversation, it's time to have the actual talk! Here's what you should do—and in what order—once this moment finally approaches:

1. Learn the other person's or people's name(s) to instantly build a connection, respect, and trust.

2. Make them the center of attention to take some of the pressure off of yourself.

3. Ask topics you're comfortable responding to if they ask you the same thing back.

4. Keep it lighthearted to make the conversation smooth and memorable.

5. Make them feel good so even if issues arise, everyone leaves feeling satisfied.

Get Their Name Right Away

Don't spend any time in the conversation worrying because you forgot the other person's name. Meeting new people can be stressful, and you might discover that you forgot their name right away as it didn't register when they were saying it. This section will include tips for remembering names so that you are able to work through any conversation.

Being good at remembering names will also help if you have to introduce this person to others later on. It's always embarrassing to have to ask them what their name is again when someone else approaches that you want to introduce them to.

Always start by asking their name. Show that you genuinely care what their name is. Oftentimes people will share it right away, but if they don't, make sure you go out of your way to acknowledge their name. This will give you the upper hand and show that you are at least trying to learn it if you do forget.

Make a comment about it, especially if you have a connection. If someone is named Willow, you might remember their name because they have similar glasses as your mom and there was a willow tree in her backyard. If someone's name is Regina, you might remember that you had a guidance counselor named Regina. Use movie and TV show characters to help you remember as well. Associate their name with someone or something right away and it will stick in your brain even better. Even if you don't remember that person's specific name, you will still be able to recall the tool you used to remember it in the first place.

Ask how their name is spelled. This is a great way to add further detail as you will have the visualization of their name's spelling in your head. If their name is Emily, you might say, "Nice to meet you, Emily. Is that with a 'y'?" They might say "yes," and then look confused, but you can follow up by saying, "Ah, I went to school with an Emilie with an 'i' and an 'e'." Some names have many different spellings, like Alissa and Alyssa, Geoff and Jeff, and Shawn and Sean. Knowing these differences can give you the chance to ask them how their name is spelled so that you have an even greater chance of remembering it when you need to the most.

Repeat their name back to them. This can be as simple as saying, "Nice to meet you, Greg!" You could also slip it in later in the conversation, by saying something like, "I really like your dress, Sharon."

This is a method to ask their name in a playful and non-awkward manner if you did forget. You can say, "Can I get you a drink, Susan? It was Susan, right?" She might say, "Sarah actually," but you can laugh it off. Now there's an even higher chance of you remembering her name since you had the mix up anyway!

Make Them the Center of Attention

When all else fails, remember that most people like talking about themselves. It's a topic we're all comfortable discussing because it's what we know the most about. You could talk about yourself all day and not in an egotistical way; simply because you know the most information about yourself. You are able to form your own opinions as thoughts come to you, meaning there isn't as much investigation required versus how you might try to get to know someone else.

Make the other person feel special and choose words that give them confidence. Who do you enjoy being around the most? It's likely someone who gives you confidence and makes you feel good about yourself rather than the person who is always putting you down and making you feel small.

"It sounds like you're going through a lot," can be a way to show empathy without offering a matter-of-fact statement. You can create a summarized version of an empathetic response that encapsulates their experience to let them know that you're listening. You don't need to provide them with a huge show and display of emotion. Simply tilting your head and saying something like, "I'm so sorry to hear that," can make the person feel like they can count on you.

Ask them follow-up questions about a subject they bring up. It can make them feel smarter and lets them know you're engaged in the conversation. For example, look at this conversation between two colleagues:

- Katie: What did you do today?

- Arthur: I spent most of my day in the garden.

- Katie: Oh really? You have a garden?

- Arthur: Yeah, just a few garden boxes in my backyard. I don't have a ton of space.

- Katie: Wow, so what kind of things do you grow?

- Arthur: Mostly vegetables and a few flowers. I try to start small and buy things that are already grown at my local hardware store.

- Katie: I'd imagine that takes a lot of work. How did you learn how to garden?

As you can see, Katie didn't dive right into quizzing Arthur on every little thing he knows about gardening. She took some time to gather some facts about him, and it shows that he is opening up. In each response he shares more and more information, letting Katie know that he is consenting to share more information about his hobby. Katie can then choose many different avenues of discussion based on the questions that she asks Arthur. She could go more into what specific vegetables he grows. She might ask if it's an expensive hobby. She could ask for tips for her indoor plants. Maybe they start talking about using the vegetables and what kinds of things they like to cook. It could branch off into a whole culinary discussion, creating a cycle of more and more conversation topics.

Discover their opinion on the subject. If you show them that you're interested in hearing their specific viewpoint, it can make them more likely to feel like the center of attention. This is especially useful if you notice one person is acting quieter than others. For example, if John keeps talking over Susan, perhaps you ask Susan, "What do you think about what John said?" Have your own answer prepared so that you can quickly respond if Susan is caught off guard. By doing this, you're forcing John to also reflect and wonder if he's been talking over Susan a little too much, and you've prompted Susan so that she'll hopefully start speaking up more.

Take the details of their conversation to their past. If someone is talking about their patio herb garden, ask them when they discovered their passion. "Did you always have a vegetable garden growing up?" is a question that can have many outcomes. They might discuss their childhood, mention their family life growing up, or maybe they avoid the topic. This would then give you insight into the boundaries of the conversation.

If they're really giving you nothing, ask them if there's anything wrong. See if they'd rather sit down if you've been standing for a while. Refill their drink or consider offering a snack. Maybe they would prefer to be somewhere quieter, or perhaps stepping outside onto the patio for fresh air would change the mood. Ensure all of their basic needs have been met. If you're hosting a large party, you might have someone else grab them a meal so you can focus on other guests.

Introduce them to other people. This is like teaching them a new skill in a way. For example, you might introduce them to the bartender. You tell them that this is a friend from a long time ago and to ask them for anything they need. The rest of the night, they'll feel more comfortable in this new environment, allowing them to open up even more while feeling like you truly care about their needs.

Sometimes it's best to just walk away. Pushing someone who is too closed off can mean pushing them completely away. If someone needs space, give it to them as they'll be more likely to come back around later on.

Ask What You Would Want to Be Asked

When you ask someone a question, they might ask you the same right after, so only direct questions to them that you are prepared to answer yourself. For example, if you have divorce court and a root canal next week, it might not be the most desirable conversation to have at a business meeting. Maybe avoid asking the other person what they're up to next week because they might end up asking you the same back.

This is also a way to keep things light and help you fine tune your empathy skills. What do you wish the other person would ask? What would you be most comfortable with hearing? If you've been watching a lot of documentaries lately, you might ask them if they've seen any good ones. Not only could this lead you to add a new one to your collection, but it can give you something to talk about if you need a conversation topic.

Ask them about topics that you like as another easy go-to. Food is a common relatable experience. If you had a delicious dinner that day and want to bring it up, you can start by asking them if they've eaten anything good lately. Everyone has to eat, so most people will have an answer. They could share that their wife made a delicious homemade apple pie. You could lead into many discussions from a small statement like this alone.

Take turns answering the questions you're asking if they're not being too receptive. Also remember to give them a chance to answer no matter how eager you are to share your thoughts.

Be prepared if you don't like their response. If you ask if they've seen any good reality TV lately and they scoff by saying they hate all reality TV in general, then it's good to have a backup subject rather than launching into the latest family drama on your favorite docuseries.

Keep It Lighthearted

Don't assume the worst about the other person—always assume the best. If you get a hint they might be growing defensive or angry, wait before you react because it can be easy to misread other people, especially when first meeting them. It might take some time to warm up and get a better sense of their true personality and demeanor.

Maybe they're having a really bad day. If someone's behavior is concerning to you, check-in with someone you feel comfortable with. For example, if you're meeting with a more senior manager, your day-to-day manager might have insight into who they are as a person. You might ask if they always behave a certain way or if something happened to make them upset. This helps to prevent any future encounters that could exacerbate the issue while focusing on things that will keep the air clear.

To keep things lighthearted, insert smiles and laughter whenever you can. It is possible to smile too much, however, and it can come off as nervousness. Remember to keep a closed mouth and squint your eyes when you're intently listening to someone. Practice smiling in the mirror to help it present more naturally. Sometimes forced and fake smiles can make it appear that we're just angrily showing our teeth. This can be off-putting for the other person and will create a sense that you're just pretending to show interest.

Notice the way they might be feeling and identify triggers that are making them upset. People often look at the things that are causing them issues. Is someone grimacing because they're upset, or are they tugging at an uncomfortable blazer? Is someone actually disinterested in what you're saying, or do they keep looking at the person talking rather loudly in front of them? Examining the context of the situation will help you to identify cues into the real reasons they might be upset so that you don't interpret these discomforts as things of your own doing.

Remember there is no *winning* in a friendly conversation. The goal should be for the both of you to connect and achieve the milestones that you set for yourself. If you notice that they're trying to one-up you or contradict what you say, change the subject and let them take over the conversational reins. You don't have to start a game with them and can instead let them have their small victory. It's like someone trying to race you on the highway. After a certain point just let the other person have it because there will be no winners when both of you get a speeding ticket or cause an accident. There won't be any winners in a conversation that results in both people walking away agitated and annoyed.

Find ways to add in fun games when chatting. If you're on a first date or meeting up with friends, look at the people around you. Maybe you see a couple sitting there. You can ask the other person you're with if they think it's the couple's first date or if they've been married for years. Again, dogs are really fun conversation topics. You can count the dogs in a surrounding area with friends. There are plenty of fun icebreaker games you can play with the people around you to keep the vibes fun and playful.

Always compliment the area or the event. For some people, finding flaws comes more naturally than identifying positive factors. However, adding compliments will show that you have a positive outlook and are approachable. You might say something like, "That's an interesting carpet choice," or "I really like the light fixtures in here." This can lead to them calling out other things, which gives opportunities to keep long conversations flowing.

Apologize if a joke goes too far. It will only make things worse if you deny hurt feelings and double down. Sometimes when we try so hard to be funny, it can come out weird and not like it sounded in our head. If someone doesn't think your joke is funny, just apologize and move on rather than trying to prove to them why you think it's a good joke.

Research what they like beforehand. If you're interviewing a celebrity or meeting with an important business figure for work, you can likely find information about them online. Mentioning these things not only shows increased interest on your end, but it will also make them feel good as they'll be more comfortable talking about the things that they like.

Focusing on positive conversations is better for your health! Letting a conversation fail and being overcome by negative emotions will only set you back. This is true for both your performance at work and in relationships, as well as your overall physical and mental health (Bradberry, 2016).

Find something that is positive. There has to at least be one thing we can be grateful about. What positive spin can you put on an unexpected, shared happening? For example, if the restaurant is out of the item that your coworker wanted to order, you might make a comment about how thankful you are that they have great drinks. Look on the bright side and try to incorporate this into your conversation to keep them feeling positive and grateful as well.

Know the difference between actual issues and just imagined ones. Did someone say that they were having a terrible time, or did you just assume that based on a weird look they gave you? If you do identify a factual factor as to why there might be an issue, then you can find a practical solution. For example, if people are leaving a dying party, maybe it means you should turn on some different music or play a light game with some people to change the energy. When you find the source of the things that are giving the event a strange energy, it will be easier to determine the practical method to keep it lighthearted.

Make Them Feel Good

Your goal should never be to enter a conversation with the intention of making another person feel bad. If that is the case, then there is a deeper issue to work through first. Maybe it will require more reflection. Having a fight with a partner will require a discussion and maybe some apologies from both parties to work through a conflict. However, it shouldn't involve you wanting to make your partner feel bad. You should want to come to a conclusion that's beneficial so your partner can better understand how they might have hurt you to prevent it from happening again. If a boss cut your bonus in half and hasn't been supportive, certainly this makes you upset, but you still shouldn't go in with the goal of wanting to hurt them. This will just create a new problem while ignoring the initial issue.

When the conversation goes in a direction that makes you upset, it is still best for you if you focus on making them feel good. When someone offends you, it's fine to walk away without giving praise and compliments. However, even in times of conflict we can focus on lifting the other person up. Not only does this give you more control over the situation by allowing you to reach your specifically desired outcome, but it will also make them better after the conversation. They will attribute this healthy growth to you, and it will facilitate a more positive experience for future conflicts as well.

Withhold judgment and listen kindly to the other person while they're sharing. Even if your child is telling you about how they snuck out last night and how they wrecked their new car, you can withhold judgment until the end. If you show them that you're angry right away, they might shut down and not share the rest of the story with you, leaving out crucial details. Take a minute to work through those initial feelings so that when you return, you're prepared to find the most beneficial solution for all parties.

Show encouragement that they can keep sharing with you. Wait to give any opinions until after they've finished sharing with you, and only once they've given consent to taking on that advice. Some situations might call for only support and understanding rather than giving criticism or advice.

Sometimes it's the other person who is making the conversation uncomfortable. Perhaps they say something a little rude or make a poor choice with the joke they share. Even if their joke doesn't land, you can still at least compliment the joke by saying something like, "I like the way your mind thinks."

Show appreciation and give thanks to them for showing up and participating. This might include phrases like

- Thanks for driving all the way out here to celebrate tonight.

- I really appreciate you getting a sitter so we could have some much-needed girl time tonight.

- I'm so looking forward to having a great time tonight, I'm really glad you came.

Give unique compliments. Saying something like, "You look nice," is always a kind gesture, but more specific compliments can boost their ego. Notice the way they are wearing their hair or an outfit choice. Some examples are

- Green really is your color!

- Your hair really brings out your eyes.

- I wish I had taste as good as yours.

- You always know how to put together a gorgeous outfit.

Don't forget to compliment any part of the event that they might have helped with. This would include compliments like

- The menu is perfect for tonight.

- Everyone here is having a really great time.

- You're such a good host; I love coming to your events.

- The speeches tonight were really put together and thought provoking.

- This is such a great time that I certainly won't be forgetting soon.

Chapter 7:

After the Conversation

Improving conversation skills doesn't stop once the discussion has. You can still implement important techniques to continue your advancement through these discussions. These are

1. Prepare an exit strategy so you can leave the conversation smoothly.

2. Don't beat yourself up if the conversation doesn't go as you had wished.

3. Give yourself time to rest and decompress after big social interactions.

4. Move on afterwards since you can't go back in time. Instead, prepare for the next.

Have an Exit Strategy

Sometimes hosts don't want to be rude, so it's important to pick up on those social cues and know when it is time to go. If they are cleaning up, yawning, or even have changed into more comfortable clothes, it might be your cue to leave. It can be an awkward topic to approach, but a few phrases below might help. Try

- "What were you thinking? Did you want to have another drink, or should we head out?"

- "I was thinking about heading out soon, unless you wanted to hang longer?"

The same goes for yourself. Learning how to end a conversation will make things a lot less awkward. You might want to keep hosting the chatty friend at night who keeps pouring more wine for everyone, but you need to get to bed to work the next day!

Allow an exit strategy for the other person as well. It's good to keep a conversation going, but you don't need to start so broad with what you're discussing right off the bat. Give a quick summary and if they ask for more details, you will likely be able to naturally fall into that aspect of the conversation. But if you dive right into a very long story, you're going to lose them. They might have just arrived and need to use the restroom, or maybe they want to find a spot to take off their coat and grab a drink. Keep conversations brief and light until you get a signal from the other person that they're ready for a more intense conversation.

Use "I need" statements for getting out of the conversation. That way, the other person can't argue with you. Some people can be pushy and might not want you to leave, but if you have a physical reason to exit, they can't argue against it as easily. These include phrases like

- "I need to go check on the quiches in the oven..."
- "I need to use the restroom..."
- "I need to get the kids ready for bed..."
- "I need to go home to let the dogs out..."
- A graceful exit starts with a "thank you."

Share your reason if you want but note that it is not necessary. You don't owe anyone an explanation; it's perfectly fine to leave early if you don't feel well or just want to be alone. As much as we might need to force ourselves out of the house, especially if you're an introvert struggling with social anxiety, we still have limits and it's important to follow them and listen to our bodies. Pushing yourself too hard might mean forcing yourself back into your shell. If someone is being really pushy and aggressive with you, it's okay to be honest. Don't let them make you feel bad about the choices you're making for yourself. If they don't let up, it might just be a sign that you need to have a more serious conversation about setting boundaries with them.

If you have to leave in the middle of someone's conversation, you can share an apology as well. You don't owe them one necessarily, but it can help soften the blow if you have to interrupt a conversation to exit quickly to prevent missing a timed flight or cab. You can find a way to politely transition into this abrupt exit with phrases like

- "I'm sorry I have to go; I didn't realize how late it was!"
- "Forgive me for leaving so quickly but I have to catch my bus."
- "I really want to finish this conversation, but we'll have to pause until tomorrow."
- "I wish I didn't have to leave, but I need to get home to the babysitter."
- "Can we pick up where we left off tomorrow? I hate to go, but it's way past my bedtime and I work early tomorrow."

It can also help to add a compliment to the conversation. If someone is sharing something interesting or really opening up, it might feel almost insensitive to leave. You might compliment them by saying

- "I loved that story you shared about your mother. I want to hear the rest, so maybe we can talk on the phone tomorrow?"
- "I'm sorry to have to cut the conversation off, I appreciate that you opened up to me, but I can't miss this ride. Can we meet up for lunch next week?"

Mention the next time you might get together to add further cushion when you need to exit quickly. It shows the other person that you genuinely did enjoy their chat, and you want to put effort into meeting up again.

Don't Put Too Much Weight on the Outcome

It can feel like one simple word might have derailed the entire night if you hang too much on the conversation. Take pressure off yourself and the conversation. Don't let the weight of these small talks press down on you to the point that you're feeling more stressed. Putting this much weight on the conversation will just make you even more afraid the next time you have to conversate. To make sure you're not putting too much weight on the outcome of conversations and scaring yourself away from participating in new ones, follow these rules:

1. No one is perfect. Most of the people that you had discussions with the night before are likely going through the same thing as you. Rumination can be exhausting, but remember that people are more focused on their own flaws rather than any minor missteps you took.

2. Don't replay them over and over again. There's no point. Reliving an embarrassing moment might actually cause you to warp your own perception if you're not careful. Stick to reality, and don't let yourself cycle through endless "what ifs," because there is no going back once a conversation is over.

3. Realize the end result isn't always seen instantly. While it might not seem like that important conversation you were looking forward to had the result you expected, time will truly tell how much of an impact it made. At first, you won't see instant results, but they could come way down the line, so be patient.

4. Only cover the conversation once: don't repeatedly ruminate. The second or third time you're picking apart a conversation, it's time to stop, move on, and focus on something else. Our

brains want to do this because it feels like we're alleviating an issue, but instead what happens is that you're actually giving it too much energy, causing it to seem like a bigger deal than it is.

5. Acknowledge and confront the things you messed up on. If you did talk too much, say something offensive, or even felt like you were withdrawn all night, you can own these things so that you know what to do in the next conversation.

6. Recognize the good things that happened. Don't beat yourself up and pick out all the things that you did that were bad; take time to remember the good things you did and said so that you feel better about yourself.

7. Find something practical to improve. Once you do own those things that were less than perfect, you can find a practical way to improve. Next time, check how much you're talking to give other people a chance to speak. If you've said something offensive, apologize and keep your jokes more lighthearted. If you didn't talk enough, try to speak up and ask more questions next time.

8. Distract yourself. Sometimes the only way to avoid constant rumination is to do something distracting. Find an activity that absorbs your mind like reading, exercising, or playing a video game.

9. Avoid bringing it up again. Unless you said something horribly offensive, don't bring up old conversations. You might feel like you were awkward the other day while chatting with a friend, but there's no need to say you're sorry for that. They might not even know what you're talking about because they didn't think you were awkward. Then if you did bring that up, you end up creating an awkward situation, causing an endless cycle of uncomfortableness and regret.

10. Remind yourself of fact versus fiction. Are you basing your feelings off of things that actually happened or just feelings you perceived?

Identify things that trigger you to have these anxious feelings. Triggers are small signs that can evoke specific emotions, usually negative feelings. Did someone make a comment about your appearance, which could be one of your biggest insecurities? Did they bring up a topic dealing with a sore subject that causes you to feel vulnerable? If you can identify the things that trigger anxious feelings and endless rumination, you can be prepared to deal with those feelings as they arise.

Sometimes, the desire to avoid triggers can lead to self-sabotage. For example, if you are afraid of a date going poorly, you might cancel the date altogether. You might never go out with friends because you constantly feel triggered that no one likes you. Feeling out of control with our emotions gives this false sense that being destructive is a way to regain that power. This can lead to a negative outcome, exacerbating issues.

Focusing too much on flaws means that we lose sight of the things that are actually healthy for us, too. For example, if you think a situation went terrible when it really didn't, you might make drastic changes to yourself only to realize that you were better before, when you were truer to yourself. The intense pressure can feel like too much, and sabotaging the end result tricks us into thinking we've reached a way to get closer to overcoming those fears.

In reality, we have to be patient and learn how to improve in slow, realistic steps that will get us closer to reaching our goals. Take time to learn about the things that are making you anxious and making you feel triggered so that each conversation becomes easier, making the next one more manageable.

Take Time to Decompress

Conversations can be draining, especially important ones related to your career. Don't feel guilty about needing a break or taking time off after the conversation. Sometimes just spending time alone and taking the day off from conversations is needed to avoid burnout, especially if you're an introvert.

Some people require alone time in their daily or weekly schedule. Everyone has different preferences. If you are the total opposite and can't stand to be alone, that's even more of a sign that you should incorporate alone time into your schedule. If you don't learn how to depend on yourself, you'll never be fully cultivating a healthy level of confidence. It's also essential to avoid burnout so that you can be your best self in every social interaction. Being alone is beneficial because

- You can be free from social pressure.
- You can let your mind wander freely without having to think about anything specific.
- You can let your senses recover in a calm, nonstimulating environment.
- You can express yourself and feel free from social constraints.
- You can get to know yourself better.

To recover from intense social interactions, there are some important self-care tips that can boost your confidence and rejuvenate your social meter so that you're even more prepared for the next meetup.

Let your feelings out. Find and use whatever creative avenue helps you feel like you're doing this the best. Some people do this through art, others use music as a creative outlet. Perhaps you try writing or dabbling in every creative hobby to find the one that suits you. The more you work with your emotions, the more you control them, giving you better insight into what they mean and what they require to be managed.

Treat yourself! Buy a fancy dinner. Get a new dress. Go on a vacation after a tour of big speaking events. If you reward your efforts and practices while improving your speaking abilities, it will make you want to keep up these good habits.

Make sure your alone time is completely yours. Grocery shopping for the family alone doesn't count. Working in silence doesn't count either. Your alone time should be something fun filled with happy activities that are all your own.

Get out and do something alone, like a walk. Get rest and balance that with something healthy to do for yourself. A nap after a workout is a great balance. Walking to the park to cloud gaze is also a great way to exercise your mind and body to fill it with rejuvenating qualities.

Disconnect from the world. A lot of social interaction can make us feel drained, so unplugging for a bit can help you regain your sense of self. Turn off notifications on your phone and avoid social media during your periods of rest.

Move On and Prepare for the Next

If you fumbled, didn't say enough, or wish you had said more, chalk it up as another experience, not some life-defining moment. Sure, a conversation can change everything, but it will likely be forgotten at the end of the day. Constantly ruminating and going over everything you said in your head will only make you more anxious than when you started. You did the best you could do, and anything you're not fully proud of is simply a learning experience that will help you to do even better in the future.

We ruminate because it makes us feel like we'll find a solution to the problem we're fixated on. Instead of rumination, try to do these things

- Do a physical task like walking, cleaning, or organizing to keep your mind and body focused.

- Remember that your thoughts aren't always facts.

- Reevaluate if this problem is affecting your goals or if it needs to be incorporated with them.

- Take accountability for your feelings. Do they need to change, or do you need to change the way you interpret your feelings?

- Always remember that there's a difference in the things we want to change and the things we have the power and control to change.

Face these feelings head on and don't avoid your emotions, as this will never help you improve and instead keep you stuck in a cycle of judging yourself. While it can be hard to admit some of the things you're feeling, it's necessary to help you thrive in future situations.

Let your anxious thoughts float away like leaves on the surface of a calm stream. Picture them as a pasture of wild horses running in the distance. Your thoughts are there but they don't define who you are. It's how you choose to act on them and manage these feelings that is really telling.

Keep yourself focused on the present moment and thinking about the things that you'll achieve in the future rather than having a mindset surrounding the failures of the past.

Take action and keep looking for ways to continually improve. Reinforce the progress you've made through positive affirmations. It's a process that can be scary, but I hope at this point it's not so overwhelming. You will learn many things along the way and there will always be an opportunity for improvement. Seek out new experiences because the things you fear most when it comes to talking won't be as bad as they seem in your head.

The scariest thing of all is never letting go of these fears and being constantly held back by them throughout your life!

Conclusion

There will soon be a day when you'll get home from a long day at work, a holiday party, or just a day running errands and you will realize that you didn't struggle to converse at all. Being free from social struggles is *so* empowering. It allows you to live the life you want, not held back by the fear of judgment. Avoiding the common pitfalls that used to cause you stress and panic is life changing.

Rejection isn't as likely to happen to you as you might fear, and even in those moments you do feel cast off, your strong confidence and self-assurance will allow you to move on, preventing past conversations from becoming endless rumination.

To recap, I created a quick cheat sheet of affirmations inspired by the 31 techniques. Use this summary as a reminder of why you are so strong at holding conversations. Repeat these daily, especially while looking in the mirror, to help build your confidence. Alternatively, you can write them down on Post-its to keep in the car or place on your mirror. The possibilities are endless!

1. I am stronger than my biggest weaknesses.
2. I have many strengths, talents, and beneficial abilities.
3. I have strong goals that I work hard to achieve.
4. I am a great listener and have excellent comprehension skills.
5. I am a conversation expert and can navigate any type of conversation
6. I am overcoming my anxiety with each new conversation I have.
7. I recognize that my problems are not as big as I think they are.

8. I am good at practicing conversations.

9. I am my favorite person to have a conversation with.

10. I am a confident, independent person who is capable of having any discussion.

11. I am relaxed and don't hold any anxiety in my body when talking to others.

12. I am able to understand what somebody is saying beyond their words.

13. I am a body language expert.

14. I am an amazing host, and people love having conversations with me.

15. I am a curious and inquisitive person that other people like talking to.

16. I love hearing what other people have to say and share with me.

17. I am great at responding to people and holding an interesting conversation.

18. I am good at connecting with others.

19. I am an intelligent, knowledgeable, and smart person.

20. I am an expert on different topics in the world.

21. I navigate conversations in a healthy way.

22. I am prepared for anything that might happen.

23. I enjoy connecting with others and I love meeting new people.

24. I am fascinated by the things other people have to share.

25. I am not afraid of bringing up any topic naturally in a conversation.

26. I have a lighthearted and positive mindset.

27. I love making other people feel good

28. I am good at reading social cues.

29. I do not let my anxieties about the past hold me back.

30. I deserve relaxation and self-care.

31. I am able to move on quickly, and I'm prepared for anything.

You don't have to be perfect; each conversation will simply be a new opportunity to learn and improve! Think of it like climbing a set of stairs. Though the end of the climb might look high out of reach, remember that each stair is one step further from your past and one step closer to the future.

Start the conversation now by leaving a review! I would love to keep the conversation going so all my readers can become the best conversationalist possible!

References

Albrecht, K. (2012). The (only) 5 fears we all share. *Psychology Today*. https://www.psychologytoday.com/us/blog/brainsnacks/201203/the-only-5-fears-we-all-share#:~:text=There%20are%20only%20five%20basic,%2C%20separation%2C%20and%20ego%20death.

American Psychiatric Association. (2020). Rumination: A cycle of negative thinking. https://www.psychiatry.org/News-room/APA-Blogs/Rumination-A-Cycle-of-Negative-Thinking#:~:text=Rumination%20involves%20repetitive%20thinking%20or,and%20can%20worsen%20existing%20conditions.

Barnard, D. (2017). Exercises to warm up your voice before a speech. *VirtualSpeech*. https://virtualspeech.com/blog/exercises-warm-up-voice-before-speech?token=f9199aa423c840279976dc7a839b47e0

Bauer-Wu, S. (2013). 7 steps to relax your body. *Mindful*. https://www.mindful.org/7-steps-to-relax-your-body/?token=f9199aa423c840279976dc7a839b47e0

Bradberry, T. (2016). 3 powerful ways to stay positive. *Forbes*. https://www.forbes.com/sites/travisbradberry/2016/08/23/3-powerful-ways-to-stay-positive/?token=f9199aa423c840279976dc7a839b47e0&sh=7349486919c9

Brenner, G. H. (2017). A six stage tool to stop self-pressuring. *Psychology Today*.

https://www.psychologytoday.com/us/blog/experimentations/201711/six-stage-tool-stop-self-pressuring

Changing Minds. (n.d.). Types of conversation. http://changingminds.org/techniques/conversation/types/types.htm

Cirino, E. (2019). 10 tips to help you stop ruminating. *Healthline.* https://www.healthline.com/health/how-to-stop-ruminating?token=f9199aa423c840279976dc7a839b47e0

Cleveland Clinic. (2022). 21 tips for mindfulness. *Healthessentials.* https://health.clevelandclinic.org/what-is-mindfulness/?token=f9199aa423c840279976dc7a839b47e0

Conversation Starters World. (2022, November 25). Open-ended questions. https://conversationstartersworld.com/open-ended-questions/?token=f9199aa423c840279976dc7a839b47e0

Cuncic, A. (2022). Small talk topics. *Verywell Mind.* https://www.verywellmind.com/small-talk-topics-3024421

David, T. (2016). Boosting someone's confidence in 5 steps. *Psychology Today.* https://www.psychologytoday.com/us/blog/the-magic-human-connection/201604/boosting-someones-confidence-in-5-steps

Davis, T. (n.d.). Self-Reflection: Definition and how to do it. *Berkeley Well-Being Institute.* https://www.berkeleywellbeing.com/what-is-self-reflection.html?token=f9199aa423c840279976dc7a839b47e0

Drake, K. (2022). 9 tips to help stop ruminating. *PsychCentral.* https://psychcentral.com/health/tips-to-help-stop-ruminating?token=f9199aa423c840279976dc7a839b47e0#identify-the-source

Florida Behavioral Health. (2019). 4 ways that untreated anxiety impacts physical health. *LifeStance Health.* https://www.behavioralhealthflorida.com/blog/4-ways-untreated-anxiety-physical-health/

Gallo, A. (2011). How to build confidence. *Harvard Business Review.* https://hbr.org/2011/04/how-to-build-confidence?token=f9199aa423c840279976dc7a839b47e0

Glickman, J. (2010). Exiting a conversation gracefully. *Harvard Business Review.* https://hbr.org/2010/03/exiting-a-conversation-gracefu-2?token=f9199aa423c840279976dc7a839b47e0

Goman, C. K. (2011). The art and science of mirroring. *Forbes.* https://www.forbes.com/sites/carolkinseygoman/2011/05/31/the-art-and-science-of-mirroring/?sh=125b40ca1318

Grohol, J. (2016). Become a better listener: Active listening. *PsychCentral.* https://lah.elearningontario.ca/CMS/public/exported_courses/ENG2D/exported/ENG2DU03/ENG2DU03/ENG2DU03A02/_teacher/activelistening2.pdf

Guest Author for rtor.org (2020, January 29). Why social anxiety disorder is more and more common in our society. *Rtor.org.* https://www.rtor.org/2020/01/29/why-social-anxiety-disorder-is-common-in-our-society/

Hedges, K. (2013). The five best tricks to remember names. *Forbes.* https://www.forbes.com/sites/work-in-progress/2013/08/21/the-best-five-tricks-to-remember-names/?token=f9199aa423c840279976dc7a839b47e0&sh=12337203501f

Hoge, B. (2022). Study shows greater increase in depression and anxiety in minorities during the pandemic. *UAB News.* https://www.uab.edu/news/health/item/12841-study-shows-greater-increase-in-depression-and-anxiety-in-minorities-during-the-pandemic

Launch Digital Marketing. (2013). How to read body language – Revealing the secrets behind common nonverbal cues. *Fremont University*. https://fremont.edu/how-to-read-body-language-revealing-the-secrets-behind-common-nonverbal-cues/

Lindberg, S. (2020). Tips for goal setting. *Verywell Mind*. https://www.verywellmind.com/tips-for-goal-setting-self-improvement-4688587

MacLeod, C. (n.d.). Places where can practice making conversation and generally work on your social skills. *Succeed Socially*. https://www.succeedsocially.com/practiceconversation

Mason, S. (2010). Topics to avoid. *Psychology Today*. https://www.psychologytoday.com/us/blog/look-it-way/201001/topics-avoid?token=f9199aa423c840279976dc7a839b47e0

Mayo Clinic. (2021). Social anxiety disorder (social phobia). https://www.mayoclinic.org/diseases-conditions/social-anxiety-disorder/symptoms-causes/syc-20353561

Mind Tools Content Team. (2022, December 13). How to build self-confidence: Prepare yourself for success. *Mind Tools*. https://www.mindtools.com/ap5omwt/how-to-build-self-confidence

Morgan, P. (2021). The top 7 habits of light-hearted people. *Solutions for Resilience*. https://www.solutionsforresilience.com/light-hearted/?token=f9199aa423c840279976dc7a839b47e0

National Institute of Mental Health. (n.d.). Social anxiety disorder. https://www.nimh.nih.gov/health/statistics/social-anxiety-disorder#:~:text=An%20estimated%2012.1%25%20of%20U.S.,some%20time%20in%20their%20lives.

National Social Anxiety Center. (2021, September 24). Common therapy goals in CBT for social anxiety. https://nationalsocialanxietycenter.com/cognitive-behavioral-therapy/common-therapy-goals/

Nollan, J. (2022). How to stop putting pressure on yourself: 8 highly effective tips. *A Conscious Rethink*. https://www.aconsciousrethink.com/18435/how-to-stop-putting-pressure-on-yourself/?token=f9199aa423c840279976dc7a839b47e0

Patel, K. (2020, September 1). Are you putting too much pressure on yourself? Here's how to stop. *Mbghealth*. https://www.mindbodygreen.com/articles/how-to-stop-putting-too-much-pressure-on-yourself?token=f9199aa423c840279976dc7a839b47e0

Psychology Today. (2020, December 9). Self-Hatred. https://www.psychologytoday.com/us/basics/self-hatred

QuestionPro. (2022, October 18). Open-Ended questions: Examples & advantages. https://www.questionpro.com/blog/what-are-open-ended-questions/?token=f9199aa423c840279976dc7a839b47e0

Resilient Staff. (2018, June 13). 11 ways to decompress after high stress. *Resilient*. https://resilientblog.co/calm/11-ways-to-decompress-high-stress/?token=f9199aa423c840279976dc7a839b47e0

Sinicki, A. (2020, January 7). How to boost the confidence of others. *Healthguidance.org*. https://www.healthguidance.org/entry/14515/1/how-to-boost-the-confidence-of-others.html?token=f9199aa423c840279976dc7a839b47e0

Specktor, B. (2021, July 26). 9 magic phrases that can save awkward conversations. *Reader's Digest.* https://www.rd.com/list/conversation-skills/

Sterling, K. (2020, February 6). 16 social cues you're not picking up on at work. *Inc.* https://www.inc.com/ken-sterling/16-social-cues-youre-not-picking-up-on-at-work.html

Tarver, K. (2022, October 19). 650+ interesting questions to ask for engaging conversation. *The Pleasant Conversation.* https://thepleasantconversation.com/interesting-questions-to-ask/?token=f9199aa423c840279976dc7a839b47e0

Van Edwards, V. (2022). Mirroring body language: 4 steps to successfully mirror others. *Science of People.* https://www.scienceofpeople.com/mirroring/?token=f9199aa423c840279976dc7a839b47e0

Zoppi, L. (2021, January 6). Is it normal to talk to yourself? *MedicalNewsToday.* https://www.medicalnewstoday.com/articles/talking-to-yourself?token=f9199aa423c840279976dc7a839b47e0

Printed in Great Britain
by Amazon